THE JESUS BOOK

THE JESUS BOOK

COMPILED AND EDITED BY
MICHAEL F. Mc CAULEY

The Thomas More Press / Chicago

Many friends, relatives, acquaintances and complete strangers helped in the preparation of this volume. Lest I overlook one inadvertently, I refrain from naming any. I am grateful for their assistance. Several libraries and a few bookstores tolerated my browsing through their stacks in search of obscure and not so obscure quotations. Also I am grateful to Gabrielle and her enchanted typewriter. Only once during the typing of the manuscript did it require a complete overhaul.

M.F.M.

ACKNOWLEDGEMENTS

Many of the works from which selections herein are taken are protected by copyright and may not be reproduced in any form without consent of the publishers. Every effort has been made to trace the ownership of all materials in this book and to obtain the necessary authorization for their use. If any errors or omissions have occurred in this regard, corrections will be made in all future editions. The author wishes to thank the following for permission to include selections of copyrighted material:

The Devin-Adair Co., Old Greenwich, Connecticut: "Blue Crucifixion" by Gerson de Souza in GENIUS IN THE BACKLANDS, Selden Rodman. Copyright © 1977 by Selden Rodman.

Leeds Music Ltd., London, England: JESUS CHRIST SUPERSTAR, words and music by Andrew Lloyd Webber and Tim Rice. Copyright © 1969 by Leeds Music Limited, London, England. Sole selling agent Leeds Music Corporation, NYC, for North, South and Central America. Used by permission. All rights reserved.

Simon & Schuster, Inc.: THE LAST TEMPTATION OF CHRIST by Nikos Kazantazkis. Copyright © 1960 by Simon & Schuster, Inc. Translated from the Greek by P. A. Bien. All rights reserved.

University of Colorado Press: Excerpt from "The Fair" in RAINER MARIA RILKE: VISIONS OF CHRIST, A POSTHUMOUS CYCLE OF POEMS, edited with an introduction by Siegfried Mandel, poems translated by Aaron Kramer. Copyright © 1967 by University of Colorado Press, Boulder, Colorado.

All we want in Christ, we shall find in Christ. If we want little, we shall find little. If we want much, we shall find much; but if, in utter helplessness, we cast our all on Christ, He will be to us the whole treasury of God.

Henry Benjamin Whipple
1822-1901

INTRODUCTION

JESUS is an inescapable presence in Western culture. He surfaces in every age. At times he is denounced, at other times adored. He has been the focus of compelling disputes but he has also been treated as mere window dressing. One age envisions him as an austere ascetic while another proclaims him the triumphant Pantocrator with terrible swift sword. Art, literature, music, architecture all bear his imprint. Always he is present, integral to our culture, influencing even the calendar by which we mark the years. Sooner or later, everyone confronts Jesus—Christians, Jews, Moslems. Not even the ill-fated historical quest has turned him out. Though God has been rumored to be dead, Jesus lives on.

Spared an untimely death, however, Jesus has suffered relentless dismemberment at the hands of countless interpreters. Each generation is eager to expose the "reality of Jesus for today's world." The result is many Jesuses. Man of Sorrows. Good Shepherd. Lamb of God. Bridegroom. Suffering Servant. Divine Physician. Sacred Heart. King of Glory. Alpha and Omega. Son of God. In our day, one manifestation competes with pop-culture heroes; another sweetly smiles his benediction on the just from his lowly birthplace; yet another scowls at the uproar that permeates his now secularized church.

For some, the Jesus of institutional religion is totally inadequate. A myopic romantic, a self-effacing visionary, this Jesus meekly turns the other cheek when confronted by aggression. Hopelessly callow, this Jesus is too good to be true. In his place have popped up, almost simultaneously, the Superstar and the guileless flower child. Not unlike an existentialist anti-hero, the Superstar Christ achieves authenticity and personal integrity by damning life's absurdities and making the ultimate sacrifice. The flower-child Jesus, on the other hand, is open, direct, gentle, ingenuous—perhaps even a bit naive—yet somehow refreshing alongside the remote, demythologized "ground of our being."

Not only is there a Superstar Christ and a flower-child Jesus; a Marxist-spouting Jesus makes an appearance. He challenges the age-old apolitical Savior who did not bother with Caesar's affairs so long as they did not conflict with God's domain. To his followers, Comrade Jesus preached proletarian revolt. He organized the oppressed—exploited laborers, social outcasts and political extremists. In the end, he was betrayed by his more respectable followers who found the master's infatuation with the poor and lowly rather tiresome. Comrade Jesus ended up on the cross, the victim of bourgeois treachery.

Revolutionary ideals have also given us a guerrilla Jesus, created in the image and likeness of Che Guevara. Wearing the equivalent of first century Palestinian fatigues, this Jesus is a shrewd Zealot, determined to marshal his brothers in a resistance against the Roman occupying force. His crime, the reason for his death: sedition. This Jesus dared to utter political rebellion—not the blasphemy which so outraged some of his religious contemporaries.

These two violent Jesuses are at odds with the nonviolent Christ of the all but extinct peace movement. To pacifists, Jesus successfully transcended the violence of this world; he refused to respond in kind. Exuding inner strength and depth of character, this Jesus rebukes the fiery Peter, rejects a militaristic Messiah role, and becomes the docile, yet morally courageous lamb before bureaucratic slaughterers.

Typically, Jesus has even been accused of plotting his crucifixion as a ruse, a drug-induced "death" that would trick his executioners and ultimately give him the upper hand. The unplanned thrust of a Roman's lance foiled Jesus' scheme and left the apostles—in disarray and leaderless confusion—to cover for his miscalculation, conning the whole of Western civilization for nearly twenty centuries.

It goes on and on, a different Jesus for everyone's needs—real or imagined. Jesus shows up as a social deviant who threatened an orderly society. Jesus the Black Messiah instructs black folk to stand up to and overcome whitey. Jesus the dedicated feminist preaches women's liberation to a patently patriarchal society. One scenario makes Jesus out as an active homosexual, announcing a literal understanding of brotherly love. Another shows Jesus engaging in bisexuality—a Palestinian playboy complete with de rigueur philosophy. As the *Christus,* Jesus is little more than a code name for a potent, hallucinogenic mushroom used in bizarre sexual rites. There is even an astronaut Jesus—one small step for a god; one giant leap for mankind.

Despite these many Jesuses—curious, im-

probable, extremist, ludicrous though they may be, and these in no way exhaust the variety of Jesus images over the last 2000 years—each one reveals an attempt to come to terms with who Jesus was. To some they are ridiculous, impious, even blasphemous. Yet each portrayal of Christ, in whatever faltering way, is a compliment—often backhanded—to Jesus, son of Mary, the Nazarene who, after all, was misunderstood even by his kinsfolk.

Some images of Jesus—too many—are obvious rip-offs of the traditional Christ. The now-legendary "Jesus Jeans" blatantly informed, "Thou shalt not have any other jeans but me." Jesus watches, T-shirts, posters and so on. Jesus as the endorsement of a particular ideology lends an almost universally acknowledged, awesome authority, a compelling moral imperative to any and every cause that drafts his likeness.

Yet the alternative to many Jesuses—reducing him to one acceptable image, unerringly formulated with theological precision and enforced with inquisitional authority—effectively exiles Christ to a quiet niche in the recesses of the subconscious. One and only one Jesus deflates his personality, destroys his vitality. The fascination, the invitation to explore anew his story is canceled by absolute fiat. Jesus becomes a quaint curiosity, the subject of scholarly research, but denied a flesh and blood existence. The halo surrounding this one-dimensional, officially sanctioned Christ blinds any pilgrim. He becomes unknowable, unreachable, unreal.

What follows are some of the myriad Jesuses history has yielded in the 2000 years since his birth. Quotations from the New Testament have purposely been omitted; it is, in a fashion, the primary source of feeling, impression, reflection about Jesus. No effort has been made to exclude "heretics", nor is there an embarrassing abundance of "canonized" views. Likewise, no

judgment has been made on the merit or absurdity of any opinions regarding Jesus included in this volume. The quotations collected here speak of Jesus, his work, his impact, his message as twenty centuries of men and women have perceived him. This is Jesus through others' eyes—believers, nonbelievers, agnostics, mystics, heretics.

The often contrasting depictions of Jesus in these pages are admittedly subjective. Yet they provide a sampling of the spectrum of theology, myth and tradition that attends the Jesus to which we Christians attach ourselves. It is hoped that one quote will interact with an adjacent one to highlight, nuance, clarify facets of Jesus. Understandably, some quotations may infuriate or outrage; others may inspire or challenge. Ultimately, by experiencing a variety of portrayals of Jesus, it might become easier to appreciate the meaning of Jesus in our own lives.   □

THE JESUS BOOK

I feel his brotherly hand which grasps mine, so that I can follow him. It is *not* the hand of the Messiah, this hand marked with scars. It is certainly not a *divine,* but a *human* hand in the lines of which is engraved the most profound suffering. . . . The faith of Jesus unites us, but faith in Jesus divides us.

Schalom Ben-Chorin
1967

Whereas some are led by Christ as the "shepherd" because they are capable of being guided and the part of their soul which is outside reason is tranquil, others come to him as the "king", who rules over the rational spirit and raises it up to worship God. But there are also differences among those who are under his sovereignty, depending on whether a man is ruled over mystically with in expressible mystery, according to God's fashion, or in a lesser way. I would say that those who attain to the sight of incorporeal things . . . are removed outside all matters of the senses by the "Word".

They are ruled royally by the guidance of the Only-Begotten. However, those who only penetrate as far as the world of sensual things and reverence the Creator through these, are also ruled by the Word and to the same degree stand under the Lordship of Christ. But let no one take offence if we distinguish aspects of the Redeemer in this way, and think that as a result we are transferring a division into his being.

Origen
185-253

I says, "What's this call, this sperit?" An' I says, "It's love. I love people so much I'm fit to bust, sometimes." An' I says, "Don't you love Jesus?" Well, I thought an' thought, an' finally I says, "No, I don't know nobody name' Jesus. I know a bunch of stories, but I only love people."

John Steinbeck
1902-1968

14

Man at the end of the Middle Ages turned from Christ in glory, from Christ the Teacher, to the Infant Christ, Christ working, healing, suffering, dying, and conquering death.

André Rayes
1969

Today, when we stand beneath the Christmas tree celebrating the birth of Christ, we are really celebrating the arrival on Earth of an alien and distant god or demigod thousands of years ago. When at Easter we celebrate his entombment and resurrection, we are really remembering the transformation and ascension of some of our true ancestors. Perhaps they deserve to be remembered because they have helped our Earth—then again, perhaps they don't.

Gerhard Steinhäuser
1975

15

From Bethlehem to Calvary
   the Saviour's journey lay;
Doubt, unbelief, scorn, fear and hate
   beset Him day by day,
But in His heart He bore God's love
   that brightened all the way.

              Meredith Nicholson

16 The story of Christ crucified was kept alive by word of mouth in the early Christian churches and homes. It was not until the fifth and sixth centuries that the first crucifix appears, and, then, for a very long time, the figure of Christ on it was not Christ crucified but Christ risen from the dead. Actual devotion to the Passion of Jesus did not begin until the thirteenth century, after which, the subject of the crucifixion in religious art increases in frequency during the transition from the Sienese primitives to Giotto and the later Florentine schools.

              P. J. Smith
              1950

17

And Christ himself, who preached the life of love, was yet as lonely as any man that ever lived.

Thomas Wolfe
1900-1938

18

It was not I [Jesus] whom they struck with the reed. It was another who lifted the cross onto his shoulders—Simon. It was another on whose head they placed the thorny crown. But I was up above, rejoicing over all the wealth of the archons and the offspring of the error of their empty glory. And I was laughing at their ignorance.

The Second Testament of the Great Seth
4th century

Baidāwī said that when the Jews gathered to kill Jesus, God thereupon informed him that he would take him up to heaven. Jesus then asked his disciples which of them would be willing to have his likeness cast upon him and be killed and enter paradise. One of them accepted and God put the likeness of Jesus upon him and he was crucified. It is said also that he was the one who betrayed Jesus.

Geoffrey Parrinder
1965

"My dear Don Angelo," he answered, "can you imagine John the Baptist offering a concordat to Herod to escape decapitation? Can you imagine Jesus offering a concordat to Pontius Pilate to avoid being crucified?"

Ignazio Silone
1936

When Christ was taken from the rood,
   One thorn upon the ground,
Still moistened with the Precious Blood,
   An early robin found,
And wove it crosswise in his nest,
Where, lo, it reddened all his breast!

John Banister Tabb
1845-1909

The face of Jesus is the face that belongs to us the way our past belongs to us. It is a face that we belong to if only as to the one face out of the past that has perhaps had more to do with the shaping of our present than any other. According to Paul, the face of Jesus is our own face finally, the face we will all come to look like a little when the kingdom comes and we are truly ourselves at last, truly the brothers and sisters of one another and the children of God.

Frederick Buechner
1926-

Against this, my dear people, I shall prove to you as well as I can, and as far as my weakness allows, that if we grant them that he (Jesus) is a child of man, and if we also worship him and call him "God" and "Lord," we do not give him these titles in any peculiar way, and we do not attach to him any strange names of which they (the Jews) do not make use. But it is certain for us that Jesus, our Lord, is God, Son of God and King, prince, light of light, creator and counsellor and leader and way and redeemer and shepherd and gatherer and gate and pearl and lamp; and with many names is he named. But we shall now leave all these on one side, and prove that he is Son of God, and that he is God, who has come from God.

Aphrahat the Persian Sage
285-345

19

20

I feel if Jesus can feel hung up and forsaken and uncertain in that sense—and he's Jesus—then what about me? How can I be so certain—certain in the sense of being so secure? So I tend to think of a Jesus who has had some sense of being one with the Father, who had to grow in knowledge, and who was being led down a path, the end of which he couldn't see all that clearly.

Kenneth Woodward

I know enough about the preachings of Christ. My concept of him is that he was a great revolutionist. His doctrine was devoted to the poor, the humble, to combat injustice and humiliation of the human being. I say there is a great deal in common between the spirit and the essence of Christ's teachings, and socialism.

Fidel Castro
1927–

I am no more of a Christian than Pilate was, or you are, gentle hearer; and yet, like Pilate, I greatly prefer Jesus of Nazareth to Amos or Caiaphas; and I am ready to admit that I see no way out of the world's misery but the way which would have been found by his will.

George Bernard Shaw
1856-1950

O blessed God, O Savior sweet,
    O Jesus, look on me!
O Christ, my King, refuse me not,
    Though late I come to Thee!

I come to Thee, confounded quite
    With sorrow and with shame,
When I beheld Thy bitter wounds
    And knew I did the same.

Nicholas Postgate
17th century

Christ has two natures. What does that mean to me? If it brings with it this name, Christ, glorious and consoling, it is on account of the service and the hard task he undertook for me; this it is that gives him his name. That he should be by nature God and Man is his concern. But that he should have consecrated his service, that he should have poured out his love in becoming my Savior and my Redeemer, in this do I find my consolation and my good. To believe in Christ is not to know that he is a Person who is both man and God; that avails nothing to anyone. It is to believe in that Person as Christ; that he came from God and came into the world. This is the service from which his name derives.

Martin Luther
1483-1546

Christ is the best husband.

Augustine
354-430

There could have been an attempt to revive Jesus, which necessitated that he should still be alive when taken down from the cross. . . . The body of Jesus would then have secretly been taken from the tomb on Saturday night, and not returned to it when it was found that he was too far gone to recover. On this view, when Jesus had expired, his corpse was hastily buried in a new grave whose whereabouts, like that of Moses, was never subsequently revealed.

Hugh Schonfield
1974

On the eve of the Passover, Jesus of Nazareth was hung. During forty days a herald went before him crying aloud: "He ought to be stoned because he has practiced magic, has led Israel astray and caused them to rise in rebellion. Let him who has something to say in his defense come forward and declare it." But no one came forward, and he was hung on the eve of the Passover.

Talmud
5th-6th century

Because Jesus, without office or title, acted as though he himself stood in God's place, he was crucified by those who, with office and title, were appointed to watch over the will of God. Jesus' claim was the cause of his death.

Heinz Zahrnt
1960

23

The whole of the Old Testament is gathered up in Jesus. He himself embodies in his own person the status and destiny of Israel, and in the community of those who belong to him that status and destiny are to be fulfilled—no longer in the nation as such.

J. W. Wenham
1972

24

This is my curse. Since my disciples, led
to folly by vainglorious boasts of faith,
plundered my body from the pit of death,
there's been no place where I could lay my head.
As long as stars will find their brightness pearled
in every brook, as long as sunlight calls
the spring to come back with its bacchanals,
so long must I keep wandering through the world.
From rood to rood I travel, penance-bound:
each time men drive a cross into the ground,
once more—in bloody shoes—I seek that mound;
the agony of old returns to hound
and humble me; a nail grows from each wound;
the minutes fasten me unto the rood.
Thus, every dying, endlessly renewed,
I live: each day another cross to bear;
impaled here in the chill of churches, there
in the profane booth of a gaudy fair;
strengthless today, yet plied with sickening prayer;
strengthless tomorrow, mocked at everywhere;
strengthless forever in the morning gold

of crossroads just as in the chapel cold.
I drive, a dying leaf, the wide world through.
You know the myth of the Eternal Jew?
I am myself that Ahasueras old
who dies each day, that each day he may live;
a dark, wide sea's my yearning; I can give
no coin to comfort it, nor a tomorrow.
Thus they avenge themselves, who came to sorrow
through what I told them. Martyred for my sake,
an endless legion follows in my wake.
Listen! their tread!—the clamor that they make! . . .

But no less mighty a revenge is mine:
I know the grapes are crushed at harvest-time
so that the burning juice of the red vine
may bring to men the joy for which they pine.
My blood keeps flowing from the wounds forever,
and all, believing that my blood is wine,
pour down their throats my venom and my fever . . .

Rainer Maria Rilke
1875-1926

25

Jesus, lover of my soul,
  Let me to Thy bosom fly,
While the nearer waters roll,
  While the tempest still is high.

Charles Wesley
1707-1788

26 We represent the body of Christ to ourselves as endowed with every strength and every refinement. A nature robust and sensitive, entirely free from that effeminacy to which pious imagery is so addicted; the ideal embodiment, the absolute fulfillment of all the desires of the human species, transfigured by a divine alliance: that is what our devotion loves to believe; that is what reason dares to affirm. And what a delight it is to find in the best Christian memorials the confirmation of our expectations.

A. D. Sertillanges
1932

This I know full well now, and did not know then, that the Catholic Church allows no image of any sort, material or immaterial, no dogmatic symbol, no rite, no sacrament, no saint, not even the blessed Virgin herself, to come between the soul and its Creator. It is face to face, "solus cum solo", in all matters between man and his God. He alone creates; He alone has redeemed; before His awful eye we go in death; in the vision of Him is our eternal beautitude.

John Henry Newman
1801-1890

Therefore our faith is in the one God, the Father, the Ruler of all, and in his Son our Lord Jesus Christ and in the Holy Spirit. This (= these three) from the unity of the one Godhead, the one Dynamis, the one hypostasis, the one substance, the one praise, the one rule, the one kingdom, the one image of the triad which is one in substance "by whom everything came into being."

Marcellus of Ancyra
c.360

Take, then, your paltry Christ,
    Your gentleman God.
We want the carpenter's son,
    With his saw and hod.

Francis Adams
1862-1893

[Jesus'] hearers were amazed by the authority with which He spoke. He dominated the crowds, and He was, without even striving for mastery, easily the Master of His band of disciples. Yet He constantly insisted that He was the servant of all, and as constantly demonstrated the genuineness of that strange claim. . . . The religious authorities were horrified by the freedom with which He criticized doctrines and practices hallowed by centuries of pious observance. . . . The rank and file of the Jewish nation were estranged in the end by His lack of patriotism. Yet He wept over the impending fate of Jerusalem; and He was executed as a political agitator along with two rebels against Rome. . . .

T. W. Manson
1964

[Jesus] told me that this Heart was to be honored under the form of a heart of flesh, the picture of which he wished me to be exposed and worn by me on my heart.

Margaret Mary Alacoque
1647-1690

28

Although Jesus rejected the way of violence, which his compatriots followed to their own destruction, he was actually crucified as a revolutionary. This is one of the great paradoxes of history. Perhaps the authorities feared him because they could not believe that a man with such a large popular following could have no political program. Jesus' avowed allegiance to the God of Israel, his detachment from Jewish and Roman leaders alike, did not fit into any conventional pattern. He was not even a pacifist holy man of the usual type. His opponents were baffled.

Sherman E. Johnson
1957

Christ is the world's Redeemer,
The lover of the pure,
The fount of heavenly wisdom,
Our trust and hope secure;
The armor of His soldiers,
The Lord of earth and sky;
Our health while we are living,
Our life when we shall die.

Columba
521-597

Why was he wounded on the side near the Heart? In order that we may never tire of contemplating his Heart.

Albertus Magnus
1206-1280

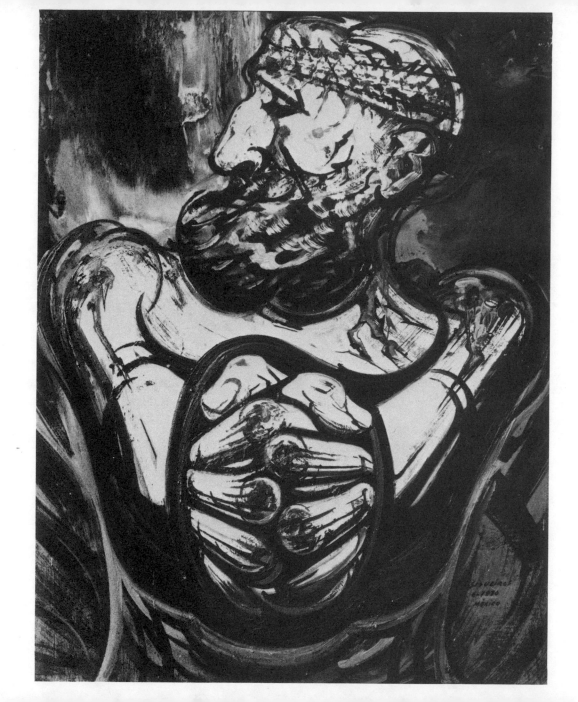

29

If there is confusion today about the divinity of Jesus, it can only be because the New Testament teaching about Jesus is not being taken seriously enough. . . . If Jesus *is* Lord, then the world just isn't the same as it was before he began exercising lordship.

Eugene H. Maly
1920–

At the moment of His death, Christ was annihilated in His soul and was deprived of any consolation and relief, since His Father left Him in the most intense aridity. . . . This was the greatest desolation that He suffered in the lower part of His human nature during His stay on earth . . . at the moment and time when this Lord was most completely annihilated in everything, namely, with respect to the esteem of man . . . with respect to nature, because by dying He annihilated Himself in it; with respect to the protection and spiritual consolation of the Father since at that time He abandoned Him . . . reduced, as it were, to nothing.

John of the Cross
1542-1591

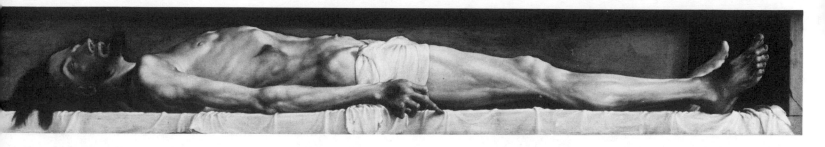

Through the Gospel of St. John my memory retained a fairly complex image of Jesus: convincing and near, like that of St. Francis of Assisi, yet, curiously hazy in this text where John refers to himself only as "He whom Jesus loved." I remembered the sellers of doves driven from the Temple, and certain phrases which made the Gospel a sort of incantation: ". . . for his hour was not yet come. . . ." "Can a devil open the eyes of the blind?" and the dark tone of "Father, deliver me from this hour. . . ." and the words spoken to Judas, "That thou doest, do quickly." . . .

Andre Malraux
1901-1976

Once in royal David's city
    Stood a lowly cattle shed,
Where a Mother laid her Baby
    In a manger for his bed:
Mary was that Mother mild,
Jesus Christ her little Child.
        Cecil Frances Alexander
        1848

Christ is the Answer.
        popular among Jesus People
        1970s

Here, in the tiny mushroom, was God manifest, the "Jesus" born of the Virgin "the image of the invisible God, the first-born of all creation" . . . in him all the fulness of God was pleased to dwell....

John M. Allegro
1923–

The personality of Jesus is richer than what even the inspired authors wrote about Him. He out-distances the experiences of Him enjoyed by His saints, and all their expressions about Him. The role of the gospels therefore is *neither* to present the reflections of a community which have no basis in the historical personality of Jesus, *nor* to provide an exhaustive description of Jesus and His actions. Rather, by placing us in communion with the inspired witnesses to Jesus and by generating in us faith in and love toward Him, they offer us the milieu of an encounter with Him which both embraces the content and surpasses the limitations of His historical life, of the experience and expression of the first witnesses and of ourselves.

Edward Malatesta
1969

In the radical Christian vision . . . we invariably find the prophetic judgment that the Jesus of the Christian tradition is alien and lifeless, having been born only by means of a negation of the original Jesus, and therewith having evolved to the very opposite of his original identity. Moreover, the radical Christian insists that Jesus can never be manifest as the man whom his disciples knew, that Jesus died on the cross; and while an image of the dead Jesus has been perpetuated by Christian orthodoxy, albeit in the mask of the God-man or the eternal Word, the true Jesus has passed through his death from a particular to a universal form, and continues to be present in a forward moving and transfiguring Word.

Thomas J. J. Altizer
1966

Jesus is the best trip.

popular saying among Jesus Freaks
late 1960s

Jesus is the Black Christ! . . . By becoming a black man, God discloses that blackness is not what the world says it is. . . . The Black Christ is he who threatens the structure of evil as seen in white society, rebelling against it, thereby becoming the embodiment of what the black community knows it must become.

James H. Cone
1938–

33

Christ is the bread for men's souls. In Him the Church has enough to feed the whole world.

Ian Maclaren
1850-1907

Perhaps the most crucial consideration we can make about the Gospels and the early church is that the portrait of Jesus handed on to us is truly credible—credible in the sense that it faithfully conveys to us who Jesus was and what he was about, credible in the sense that this portrait reveals the Risen Lord who is with his church for all times and in all places.

Donald Senior
1975

The Latin American man's devotion is toward a helpless Christ. . . . A man who is all man does not follow nor take anything from a helpless man. He protects him, he pities him, he cries for him . . . never, as far as I know, does he depict Him as in the Apocalyptic vision—the great Conquerer riding a great white stallion.

Leo T. Mahon
1962

[The Savior] is crucified as man and glorified as God. . . . We do not say this because we believe that God is one (person) and man another, and make two persons in the one Son of God, as falsely does the new heresy. Rather, one and the same is both Son of God and Son of Man, and whatever he says we refer on the one hand to his divine glory and on the other to our salvation.

Jerome
340-420

34

If we understand what prayer really is, we shall know that we may never pray to anything generated—not even to Christ—but only to God and the Father of all, to whom even Our Savior Himself prayed, as we have already said, and teaches us to pray. For when He is asked, *Teach us to pray,* He does not teach how to pray to Himself, but to the Father, and to say: *Our Father, who art in heaven,* and so on. For if the Son . . . is distinct from the Father in nature and person, then we must pray either to the Son and not to the Father, or to both, or to the Father only. Everyone will agree that to pray to the Son and not to the Father would be very strange, and maintained against the clearest evidence; and if to both, then we must obviously pray and make our requests in the plural. . . . But this is incongruous, nor can anyone point out where anyone has used it in Scripture. There remains, then, to pray to God alone, the Father of all, but not apart from the High Priest who was appointed with an oath by the Father.

Origen
185-253

Son of Life, Son of Immortality who is in the light, Son, Christ of Immortality, our Redeemer; give us power, for they seek to kill us.

Letter of Peter to Philip
4th century Gnostic document

Jesus was the final prophet who pointed out the religious dimension of everyday life. He lived an ordinary life in many respects, yet in that ordinary life he could reveal the presence of the divine and help us to appreciate the religious dimension that is part of life.

John F. O'Grady
1973

The prophecies are the strongest proof of Jesus Christ. It is for them also that God has made most provision; for the event which has fulfilled them is a miracle existing since the birth of the church to the end. So God has raised up prophets during sixteen hundred years, and, during four hundred years afterwards, he has scattered all these prophecies among all the Jews, who carried them into all parts of the world. Such was the preparation for the birth of Jesus Christ, and, as his Gospel was to be believed by all the world, it was not only necessary that there should be prophecies to make it believed, but that these prophecies should exist throughout the whole world, in order to make it embraced by the whole world.

Blaise Pascal
1623-1662

L. Fujita 66

The Qur'an itself . . . does not only or even most commonly call Jesus a prophet. He is called Messiah eleven times, and many other titles are bestowed upon him. In the Bible John the Baptist was said to be "more than a prophet," and in the Qur'an Jesus is much more.

Geoffrey Parrinder
1965

38 The holiest of men still need Christ as their Prophet, as "the light of the world." For he does not give them light but from moment to moment; the instant He withdraws, all is darkness. They still need Christ as their King, for God does not give them a stock of holiness. But unless they receive a supply every moment, nothing but unholiness would remain. They still need Christ as their Priest, to make atonement for their holy things. Even perfect holiness is acceptable to God only through Jesus Christ.

John Wesley
1703-1791

For two reasons He is called a Priest: first, because He offered up His body as an oblation and victim to God the Father for us; second, because through us He condescends day after day to be offered up. He is the Way along which we journey to our salvation; the Truth, because He rejects what is false; the Life, because He destroys death. He is the Vine, because He spread out the branches of His arms that the world might pluck in clusters the grapes of consolation from the cross.

Niceta of Remesiana
5th century

Shepherd! that with Thine amorous, sylvan song
Hast broken the slumber that encompassed me,
Who mad'st Thy crook from the accursed tree,
On which Thy powerful arms were stretched so
    long!
Lead me to mercy's ever-flowing fountains:
For Thou my Shepherd, guard, and guide shalt be;
I will obey Thy voice, and wait to see
Thy feet all-beautiful upon the mountains.
Hear Shepherd! Thou who for Thy flock art dying,
Oh, wash away these scarlet sins, for Thou
Rejoicest at the contrite sinner's vow.
Oh wait! to Thee my weary soul is crying,
Wait for me! Yet why ask it, when I see,
With feet nailed to the cross, Thou'rt waiting still
    for me!

       Lope de Vega
       1562-1635
       translated by Henry W. Longfellow

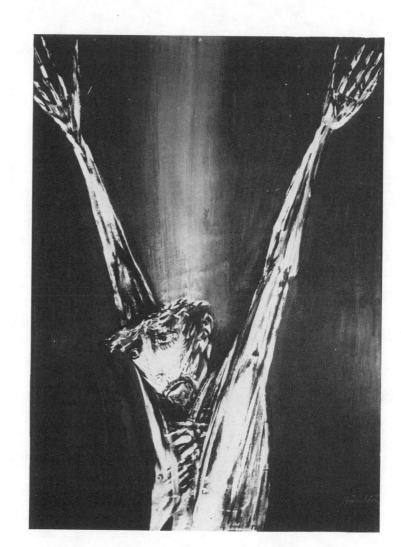

39

Harken this word, be warned by this one case;
The lion lies in wait by night and day
To slay the innocent, if he but may.
Dispose your hearts in grace, that you withstand
The Fiend, who'd make you thrall among his band
He cannot tempt more than beyond your might;
For Christ will be your champion and knight.

Geoffrey Chaucer
1340-1400

The Lord Jesus Christ, in his divine nature, is *not* "God the Son", but the one only indivisible and undivided God, in all his fullness. If the term above had been the proper expression to describe Christ's divinity, it would certainly have been used; but it is not found in the Bible. There is no reasonable explanation of this omission, except this, that he is *not* "God the Son", which is an epithet of man's device.

Robert D. Weeks
1880

Those who know only Jesus Christ and Jesus Christ crucified and who, thinking that the Word made flesh is all there is to the Word, know Christ only according to the flesh; such is the mass of men who are considered to be believers.

Origen
185-253

God, who had fashioned time and space in a clockwork of billions of sun and stars and moons, in the form of His beloved Son became a human being like ourselves. On this microscopic midge of planet He remained for thirty-three years. He became a real man, and the only perfect one. While continuing to be the true God, He was born in a stable and lived as a workingman and died on a cross. He came to show us how to live, not for a few years but eternally.

Fulton Oursler
1949

40

Sweet Robin, I have heard them say
That thou wert there upon the day
That Christ was crowned in cruel scorn,
And bore away one bleeding thorn;
That so the blush upon thy breast
In shameful sorrow was imprest,
And thence thy genial sympathy
With our redeemed humanity.

William Croswell Doane
1832-1913

O Christ, I see thy crown of thorns in every eye, thy
bleeding, naked, wounded body in every soul; thy
death liveth in every memory; thy crucified Person is
embalmed in every affection; thy pierced feet are
bathed in everyone's tears; and it is my privilege to
enter with thee into every soul.

Thomas Traherne

Every passage in the history of our Lord and Savior
is of unfathomable depth, and affords inexhaustible
matter for contemplation. All that concerns Him is
infinite, and what we first discern is but the surface
of that which begins and ends in eternity.

John Henry Newman
1801-1890

41

Christ has brought the kingdom of God nearer to
earth; but he has been misunderstood; and in place
of God's kingdom the kingdom of the priest has
been established among us.

Immanuel Kant
1724-1804

Jesus died too soon. He would have repudiated His
doctrine if He had lived to my age.

F. W. Nietzsche
1844-1900

42

Jesus was the greatest religious genius that ever lived. His beauty is eternal, and his reign shall never end. Jesus is in every respect unique, and nothing can be compared with him. . . . All history is incomprehensible without Christ.

Ernest Renan
1823-1892

JUDAS:
Jesus! You've started to believe
The things they say of you
You really do believe
This talk of God is true
And all the good you've done
Will soon get swept away
You've begun to matter more
Than the things you say

Tim Rice

Christ stimulates us, as other great men stimulate us, but we find a power coming from Him into our lives that enables us to respond. That is the experience that proves Him to be the universal spirit. It does not happen with others.

William Temple
1881-1944

Whether you think Jesus was God or not, you must admit that he was a first-rate political economist.

George Bernard Shaw
1856-1950

. . . the greatest, purest, truest socialist the world has ever seen, was our Lord and Savior Jesus Christ.

Archibald McCowen
1894

44 In politics He was a leveller or communist; in morals He was a monk; He believed that only the poor and despised would inherit the Kingdom of God.

W. Winwood Reade
1872

The Lord from Heaven,
Born of a village girl, carpenter's son,
Wonderful, Prince of Peace, the mighty God.

Alfred Tennyson
1809-1892

His parentage was obscure; His condition poor; His education null; His natural endowments great; His life correct and innocent; He was meek, benevolent, patient, firm, disinterested, and of the sublimest eloquence.

Thomas Jefferson
1743-1826

An atheist who takes his life and his work for his beloved movement really, "deadly" seriously, cannot be undermined by any cyncism or by opportunist considerations and can recognize that Jesus' victory was one of the greatest moments in the history of mankind and humanity, as Peter discovered . . . and that Jesus is still the victor.

Milan Machovec
1972

Jesus is weary with his journey that he may refresh the weary; he desires to drink when about to give spiritual drink to the thirsty; he was hungry when about to supply the food of salvation to the hungry; he dies to live again; he is buried to rise again; he hangs on the dreadful tree to strengthen those in dread; he veils the heaven with thick darkness that he may give light; he makes the earth to shake that he may calm it; he opens the tombs of the dead that he may show they are the homes of the living; he is made of the Virgin that men may believe he is born of God; he feigns not to know that he may make the ignorant to know; as a Jew, he is said to worship, that the Son may be worshiped as true God.

Ambrose
340-397

The Carpenter of Galilee
   Comes down the street again,
In every land, in every age,
   He still is building men.
On Christmas Eve we hear him knock;
   He goes from door to door:
"Are any workmen out of work?
   The Carpenter needs more."

Hilda W. Smith
b.1888

46

In the best sense of the word, Jesus was a radical. . . . His religion has been so long identified with conservatism—often with conservatism of the obstinate and unyielding sort—that it is almost startling for us sometimes to remember that all of the conservatism of his own times was against him; that it was the young, free, restless, sanguine, progressive part of the people who flocked to him.

Phillips Brooks
1835-1893

Jesus' mission was of a nature to break open the frozen patterns of men's lives and set them moving toward a very different future. But he did this in such a way that the dimensions of the revolution in human life he was generating could, at least for a time, remain concealed even from those who were very close to him. It was a quiet revolution. But it is of the greatest importance for the Christian church and for our whole understanding of the Christian faith that Jesus was a revolutionist. . . . (Yet Jesus) was not interested in a revolt or reformation that would run its course in a brief generation or less. His concern was for a permanent revolution, and in the few short years of his mission, in his life, death, and resurrection, he laid the foundations of that permanent revolution at such a level that, ever since, each fresh encounter of men with him has become the decisive turning point between the world of the past and God's new age.

James D. Smart
1969

God never gave man a thing to do concerning which it were irreverent to ponder how the Son of God would have it.

George Macdonald
1824-1905

The supreme miracle of Christ's character lies in this: that He combines within Himself, as no other figure in human history has ever done, the qualities of every race.

C. F. Andrews

Jesus is:
One Son, one number, one hypostasis, one nature, one God who was enfleshed from the holy virgin, one of the Trinity who was seen in the flesh. . . .

Jacob of Sarug
c.500

Rationalists renounce reason in their attempt to solve the problem of Christ. Either Christ was God or He was mad. The rationalist will not accept the former alternative, he dare not suggest the latter.

Arnold Lunn
20th century

Commander-in-chief of the Celestial Army, King of Zion, Eternal Emperor, Pontifex Maximus of the Christian Church, Archbishop of All Souls, Elector of Truth, Archduke of Glory, Duke of Life, Prince of Peace, Defender against the Gates of Hell, Conqueror of Death, Hereditary Lord of All Nations, Lord of Justice, and Head of the Sacred Council of the Heavenly Father.

Anonymous

48

The regular theme of Jesus' sayings was the kingdom, not himself as king. He was so dominated by the desire to proclaim the nearness of the kingdom and the need for repentance that he devoted scant attention to talk about himself. This failure to speak frequently and forthrightly about himself—if, indeed, it can be called a failure—tells us much about Jesus. He thought far more about God than he did about himself.

C. Milo Connick
1974

Everyone in the world is Christ and they are all crucified.

Sherwood Anderson
1876-1941

So the modern searchers-after-relevance say to Jesus of Nazareth, "But what do you have to say about peace?" And Jesus replies to them, "My Father loves you." They say to him, "What is your position on the race question?" And he responds, "You ought to rejoice over my Father's love." And they say to him, "What do you think about the ecological crisis?" And he answers, "Nothing can stand in the way of my Father's love." And the young apostles of relevance shake their heads in dismay. Clearly this strange Jewish preacher is completely out of it. He doesn't understand the issues at all. What in the world does God's generous love have to do with peace or ecology?

Andrew Greeley
1971

Christ's actions are not bound by our standards. He should *not* be acceptable to us if he can fit into a sensitivity-session concept of what is normal and "well-adjusted." The Christ of Christians is the Light of the World.

James K. Fitzpatrick
1976

I think of Jesus as a human being like myself. But we don't have to be exactly alike. I see myself as political but I don't want to say, therefore, that Jesus was a politician or political revolutionary. I am cautious of making Jesus too much like myself.

Gail Dunfey

49

If it were permitted to reason consistently in religious matters, it is clear that we all ought to become Jews, because Jesus Christ our Savior was born a Jew, lived a Jew, died a Jew, and that he said expressly that he was accomplishing, that he was fulfilling the Jewish religion.

Voltaire
1694-1778

When Jesus was born, doubtless, he cried and wept like other children, and his mother tended him as other mothers tend their children. As he grew up, he was submissive to his parents, and waited on them, and carried his supposed father's dinner to him, and when he came back, Mary, no doubt, often said: "My dear little Jesus, where has thou been?" He that takes not offence at the simple, lowly, and mean course of the life of Christ, is endued with high divine art and wisdom; yea, has a special gift of God in the Holy Ghost. Let us ever bear in mind, that our blessed Savior thus humbled and abased himself, yielding even to the contumelious death of the cross, for the comfort of us poor, miserable, and damned creatures.

Martin Luther
1483-1546

51

Dear brothers, you all know well that the Lord God and Savior Christ is Father and Son: I name him Father as the one without beginning and end who begets his aeon, Son, i.e., the will of the Father, who is neither embraced by a thought nor led to complete his works by matter which has already been explored. . . . But the Son of God, Christ, the demiurge of all things and guide towards immortality was begotten—as is said by the faith which we confess—was begotten, or rather, he himself came forth, who was constantly in the Father, to administer that which had come into being through him. In other words, he was begotten by proceeding forth in a way which causes no division. For the will is at the same time contained in his housing.

Constantine I
272-337

52

The disciples of Arius and Eunemius say that he (Christ) took a body not a soul; the divine nature, they say, takes the place of the soul. And they lower the divine nature of the Unique (Son) to the point (of saying) that he declines from his natural grandeur and performs the actions of the soul, by enclosing himself in the body and accomplishing everything to make it "subsist." Consequently, if the divinity takes the place of the soul, it (sc. the body) had neither hunger, nor thirst, nor was it tired, nor did it have need of food; for all this happens to the body because of its weakness and because the soul is not equipped to satisfy the needs which it has save according to the law of the nature which God has given it.

Theodore of Mopsuestia
c.400

But what do we say and think, what have we taught and what do we still teach? That the Son is not unbegotten, nor in any way a part of the unbegotten, nor of any ultimate substance, but that he by the will and counsel [of God] came into being as perfect God, only-begotten and unchangeable, and that before he was begotten or created or purposed or established, he did not exist; for he was not unbegotten. We are persecuted because we say "the Son has a beginning but God is without beginning." On this account we are persecuted, also because we say that he is of that which did not previously exist. And we express ourselves thus because he is neither a part of God nor of any ultimate substance. On this account we are persecuted; the rest you know.

Arius (to Eusebius)
d.336

Only-begotten Son and Word of God, Who art immortal and didst vouchsafe for our salvation to take flesh of the holy Mother of God and ever Virgin Mary, and without change didst become Man, and wast crucified, Christ God, and by death didst overcome death, being one of the holy Trinity and glorified with the Father and the Holy Ghost: save us!

> Byzantine Horologion,
> Prayer at the Office of
> the Typika
> Before 9th century

Crown Him with many crowns,
  The Lamb upon His throne:
Hark how the heavenly anthem drowns
  All music but its own.
Awake my soul, and sing
  Of Him who died for thee:
And hail Him as thy matchless King
  Through all eternity.

> M. Bridges
> 19th century

The real Jesus remains a shadowy figure (not because he was like that, but because there is no way to recover him) behind the Gospels, a mystery forever.

> David N. Freedman
> 1976

Christ either deceived mankind by conscious fraud [regarding an early end of the world]; or he was himself deluded; or he was divine. There is no getting out of this trilemma.

> J. Duncan
> 1870

Jesus in God's eyes is in the same position as Adam: He created him of dust, then said to him "Be!" and he is.

> Koran
> 651

A popular [Muslim] story . . . tells of the betrayal of Jesus by Judas, the trial, and the preparation of the cross. But then it is said that the cloud of darkness came down, God sent angels to protect Jesus, and Judas was crucified in his place. Then God caused Jesus to die for three hours, after which he was raised to heaven.

Geoffrey Parrinder
1965

Without his death [Jesus] would not have become an historical personality at all.

Julius Wellhausen
1905

As I looked at that man upon the cross . . . I knew I must make up my mind once and for all, and either take my stand beside him and share in his undefeated faith in God . . . or else fall finally into a bottomless pit of bitterness, hatred, and un-utterable despair.

S. Paul Schilling
1969

He wakes desires you never may forget;
    He shows you stars you never saw before;
He makes you share with Him forevermore
    The burden of the world's divine regret.

Alfred Tennyson
1809-1892

The Sermon on the Mount is Christ's biography. Every syllable He had already written down in deeds. The sermon merely translated His life into language.

Thomas Wright
1810-1877

It is clear that it is the human nature of the Word-God which suffered and died, because in no book of the prophets or the Gospel do we find that God himself died in the flesh, though we do find that the Son of God Jesus Christ died in the flesh. The expression that "God suffered in the flesh" is not correct.

Nestorian Patriarch Timothy
c.781

55

O Jesus, once a Nazareth boy,
And tempted like as we,
All inward foes help us destroy
And spotless all to be.
We trust Thee for the grace to win
The high victorious goal,
Where purity shall conquer sin
In Christ-like self-control.

Anonymous
early 20th century

Jesus grew up in Galilee; the difference between the religious environments of Galilee and Bethlehem had considerable importance. Bethlehem was traditional, orthodox, secure. Galilee was deeply religious, too, but it was surrounded by non-believers and Gentiles. The contrasting winds were many; they produced a gale of ideas. People were in a mood for reappraisal and self-examination. The atmosphere, if not cosmopolitan, was at least mixed.

Norman Cousins

Christ will remain a priest and king, though He was never consecrated by any papist bishop or greased by any of those shavelings; but He was ordained and consecrated by God Himself, and by Him anointed.

Martin Luther
1483-1546

We cannot know Jesus Christ by direct observation. The lapse of historical time, if nothing else, makes that impossible. We have nothing written by his hand. We are dependent on the records and reports of others and can see him only through their eyes. Some have drawn from this the conclusion that we can know very little if indeed anything about him; they have tended to reduce him, in the striking phrase of Giovanni Miegge, to the mathematical point which has position but no magnitude. Some would go even further and say it matters very little whether we know anything about him or not: what matters is the "that," that in Jesus Christ God encountered mankind, and not the "what," the exact nature or content of the encounter.

Stephen Neill
1976

57

We will make Jesus into everything possible so as not to face the one thing he is—God's challenge and invitation. In every naming of Jesus there lurks the danger that he becomes not the challenge of God who demands free response but the divine hero who rescues us. . . . Jesus the divine hero, evokes our sincerest thanks; Jesus, the divine challenge, evokes responsible action in the world.

John Shea
1975

Christ must be rediscovered perpetually. It is easy to read beautiful words of his and be moved by them, to accept him vaguely, not scrutinizing closely what has been recorded about him, preferring not to see him sharply in the clear air of truth. It is easy to keep him remote, put away in an atmosphere of unreality where his definite and practical demands to change the basis of human life can be dimmed into a kind of nebulous good will which exacts nothing in particular. But to study the records we have of him, is dismaying because what he demanded Christians do not do and have almost never done. St. Matthew says, "It is enough for the disciple that he be as his master." Christ's disciples have not been as their master. The Christian life as we see it and live it is an easy life. All this and heaven too.

Edith Hamilton
1948

The Christ of faith. Naturally he is good and just and all the rest of it, but he has nothing to do with reality. He may have some place in the realms of religious consciousness, symbolism, cult, or subjective Bible interpretation, but the historical Jesus is something entirely different. Only science can engrave his true likeness. Christian faith must reject both the Jesus of historical research and the pseudo faith which such a Jesus would imply. There is only one true Jesus Christ: the God-Man of full uncrippled Christian belief. And faith is as essential to our understanding of him as the eye is to color and the ear to sound. From the start Jesus demanded of all would-be followers a clear Yes! or No! to the demands of faith he made upon them—affirmation or rejection, not a little of each. This point is essential and needs no further illumination, though it is interesting to call attention to the complete nullity of the figure known as "the historical Jesus." When we measure it with the necessary objectiveness and by its own standards we can only be amazed that human intelligence can possibly contribute such a person with the effects that Jesus actually produced.

Romano Guardini

59

The highest service may be prepared for and done in the humblest surroundings. In silence, in waiting, in obscure, unnoticed offices, in years of uneventful, unrecorded duties, the Son of God grew and waxed strong.

Inscription in the Chapel
Stanford University

60

Thou wayfaring Jesus, a pilgrim and stranger,
    Exiled from heaven by love at thy birth,
Exiled again from the rest in the manger,
    A fugitive child 'mid the perils of earth—
Cheer with thy fellowship all who are weary,
    Wandering far from the land that they love;
Guide every heart that is homeless and dreary
    Safe to its home in thy presence above.

Anonymous

The opening in the side
    of Christ
reveals the riches of his love,
    the love of his Heart
    for us.

Anselm of Canterbury,
1033-1109

The fact is, our God Jesus Christ was conceived by Mary according to God's dispensation *of the seed of David,* it is true, but also of the Holy Spirit. He was born and was baptized, that by His Passion He might consecrate the water.

Ignatius of Antioch
2nd century

In MEMORIA de los NIÑOS de VIENA que MORIRAN de HAMBRE este AÑO 1946

INRI

O. Kokoschka

Like the jester, Christ defies custom and scorns crowned heads. Like a wandering troubadour he has no place to lay his head. Like the clown in the circus parade, he satirizes existing authority by riding into town replete with regal pageantry when he has no earthly power. Like a minstrel he frequents dinners and parties. At the end he is costumed by his enemies in a mocking caricature of royal paraphernalia. He is crucified amidst sniggers and taunts with a sign over his head that lampoons his laughable claim.

Harvey Cox
1969

61

I think when I read that sweet story of old,
  When Jesus was here among men,
How He called little children as lambs to His fold,
  I should like to have been with them then.

Jemima T. Luke
1841

Thou canst not comprehend it, thou who hast never been under the power of the God-man. It is more than teaching that he spreads over the earth: it is witchcraft that takes the mind captive. They who have been under Him, I believe, can never get free.

Henrik Ibsen
1822-1906

We hold for certain that Jesus, our Lord, is God the Son of God, King, the Son of the King, Light of Light, Creator, Counselor, Leader, Way, Savior, Shepherd, Gatherer, Gate, Pearl, and Lamp. He is thus called by many names. But leaving aside all the rest, let us show that He is Son of God, Himself God Who came forth from God.

Aphraates
4th century

It would be much easier to believe in Jesus if he were just God. But to believe in another *man,* to see our salvation depending on another man, is a hard thing for our pride-filled egos to accept.

Karen Wullenweber Hurley

What need was there for a soul, for the worship of a perfect man alongside God? John too, loudly proclaims the turth, "The Word was made flesh." This means that the Word was compounded with the flesh and certainly not with a soul . . . , rather did it unite itself with a body, so as to become one with it. For how else do we know Christ than as one Person, one composite nature (in composition) like a man, of body and soul? But if he also had a (human) soul, the impulses from God and from the soul would necessarily have conflicted. For each of the two is self-determining and strives towards different activities.

Lucian, Bishop of Alexandria
c.375

63

Jesus found himself in a certain sense close to the Zealots—as also to the Pharisees. There was for him a Zealotist temptation. But exactly for that reason he warned those to whom he found himself close of the terrible consequences of their fundamental position, which made all their efforts so questionable and ultimately caused them to be transformed from nonconformists into conformists. Their resistance became indeed finally so popular in Palestine that it required courage to criticize them for not taking their norms from the kingdom which is not of this world.

Oscar Cullmann
1970

In the beauty of the lilies Christ was
   born across the sea,
With a glory in His bosom that transfigures
   you and me;
As He died to make men holy, let us
   die to make men free.

Julia Ward Howe
1819-1910

PETER: What do I see, O Lord? Who is this above the tree [the cross], who is happy and laughs? Is it another whose feet and hands they are striking?

THE SAVIOR: He whom you see above the tree, glad and laughing, is the living Jesus. But the one into whose hands and feet they drive the nails is his fleshy part, which is the substitute . . . one made in his likeness.

The Apocalypse of Peter
4th century Gnostic manuscript

65

God had only one Son, and he was a missionary and a physician.

David Livingstone
1813-1873

To believe in Christ is to believe that God has come to earth to dwell with men. . . . In Jesus, we meet the living. Jesus is more than a religious genius or a holy man or a spiritual pioneer. To believe in Christ is to believe that the living God has come.

Earle W. Crawford

Medieval theologians, medieval divines, could leave nothing well alone. Jesus was to be born a man-God, with a human as well as a divine nature, so a masculine element was considered altogether necessary for his creation. With biblical authority, it was easy to contend that this was furnished by the Holy Spirit. But it was deemed essential to know exactly how this came about. It was held by many divines that the Holy Ghost, at the time of the Annunciation, penetrated Mary's body in an unusual way and there physically implanted the male element of Jesus' conception. There was much speculation as to the path which had been followed in this fecundation, the gestatory period which divided the Annunciation from the birth, and the precise moment during Mary's pregnancy at which God's essence became sufficiently formed to be deemed a man, and a God. The path, it was finally agreed, was through the right ear, and the gestatory period a normal nine months.

Adey Horton
1975

66

Sweet Jesus, in order to die,
You go, out of love for me,
To gain life,
Let me die, Lord, with you.

* * *

Sweet Jesus, already you have died
Out of love for me:
Have gained life for me,
Ah, let me die with you.

Alphonsus Liguori
1696-1787

Jesus Christ was the complete embodiment of the blessedness which he imparts derivatively to others. In him the union of God and man was actualized, so that we may say of him what we say of no other, that God actually existed in him and made him the Person he was. He knew no sin. Nay, he did not really suffer temptation, for, be the struggle ever so little, where there is struggle there is taint of sin. In Christ the God-consciousness was uninterrupted and complete; the finite was assumed by the Infinite. This is not to be thought of as an achievement of the man, still less as the reward bestowed upon him, rather we must see in his sinless Person the direct activity of God.

John M. Creed
1938

John, unto the multitude below in Jerusalem I am being crucified and pierced with lances and reeds, and gall and vinegar is given me to drink. But unto thee I speak. . . . Nothing, therefore of the things which they will say of me have I suffered . . . I was pierced, yet I was not smitten; hanged, and I was not hanged; that blood flowed from me, and it flowed not.

Apocryphal Acts of John
c.150

It seems, then, that the form of the earthly, no less than the heavenly Christ is for the most part hidden from us. For all the inestimable value of the Gospels, they yield us little more than a whisper of his voice; we trace in them but the outskirts of his ways.

R. H. Lightfoot

68

Our Lord Jesus Christ, my brethren, is our hero, a hero all the world wants. You know how books of tales are written, that put one man before the reader and shew him off handsome for the most part and brave and call him My Hero or Our Hero. . . . But Christ, he is the hero. . . . He is a warrior and a conqueror; of whom it is written he went forth conquering and to conquer. He is a king, Jesus of Nazareth King of the Jews, though when he came to his own Kingdom his own did not receive him, and now, his people having cast him off, we Gentiles are his inheritance.

Gerard Manley Hopkins
1844-1889

I love the name of Christ the Lord, the Man of
    Galilee,
Because He came to live and toil among the likes of
    me.
Let others sing the praises of a mighty King of
    Kings;
I love the Christ of common folks, the Lord of
    common things.

                  George T. Liddell

Middle-beings are formed when different properties are combined in one thing, for example the
properties of ass and horse in a mule and the
properties of white and black . . . in the color grey;
but no middle-being contains the two extremes in
full measure—they are there only in part. Now in
Christ there is a middle-being of God and man;
therefore he is neither fully man nor God (alone),
but a mixture of God and man.

                  Apollinarius

69

70

L. Lhermitte
1905

Let us ask ourselves candidly what would be the manner of man, the course of action, and what the reception Jesus Christ would meet with, if He came among us now, in circumstances parallel to those of His own times. He would be a working man, and He would speak with a provincial accent; He would attack the capitalist, the political economist, the Sabbatarian, and the bench of bishops; He would live at the East End among the roughs and gaol-birds of Tiger Bay, who are our lepers, and He would denounce the luxury and respectability of the West End as the formerly denounced Dives and the Pharisees. . . .

Anonymous
1872

If I have understood,
She holds high motherhood
Towards all our ghostly good
And plays in grace her part
About man's beating heart,
Laying, like air's fine flood,
The deathdance in his blood;
Yet no part but what will
Be Christ our Saviour still.
Of her flesh he took flesh:
He does take fresh and fresh,
Though much the mystery how,
Not flesh but spirit now
And makes, O marvellous!
New Nazareths in us,

Where we shall yet conceive
Him, morning, noon, and eve;
New Bethlems, and he born
There, evening, noon, and morn—
Bethlem or Nazareth,
Men here may draw like breath
More Christ and baffle death;
Who, born so, comes to be
New self and nobler me
In each one and each one
More makes, when all is done,
Both God's and Mary's Son.

Gerard Manley Hopkins
1844-1889

72

74

O, that the picture of the Christ
  Were painted clearly on the wall
Of every living room on earth,
  Where one could never fail at all
To see Him there—his gentle eyes
  Follow one throughout the days:
Surely those eyes would influence
  A family's manners, words and ways.

Grace Noll Crowell

A man who were merely a man and said the sort of things Jesus said would not be a great moral teacher. He would either be a lunatic—on a level with the man who says he is a poached egg—or else he would be the Devil of Hell. You must make your choice. You can fall at his feet and call him Lord and God. But let us not come with any patronizing nonsense about his being a great human teacher. He has not left that open to us. He did not intend to.

C. S. Lewis
1898-1963

No revolution that has ever taken place in society can be compared to that which has been produced by the words of Jesus Christ.

Mark Hopkins
1802-1887

75

I can see Him dying, loving
  Unto death on Calvary;
His dead hands still pleading, praying,
  Worn and torn for you and me!
"Brothers, will ye scorn and leave Me?
  Wist ye not my Father's plan?
He must wear a crown of sorrow
  Who would be a Son of Man."

Allen Eastman Cross
1921

The proper office of a mediator is to join opposed parties, for extremes meet in a middle. To achieve our union with God is Christ's work. . . . He alone is the perfect Mediator between God and men, forasmuch as the human race was brought into agreement with God through His death.

Thomas Aquinas
1225-1274

One may not usually imagine Jesus in football socks, as a kind of rejuvenated Uncle Mac or Player King; but we for our part have done a great deal to re-establish that very distance between God and man that Jesus came to destroy. Surely we know from His own dealings with us that the Almighty has a sense of humor—and if the Father, then why not the Son?

letter in the *Church of England Newspaper* reacting to *Godspell*
1972

Now in the month of Adar, Jesus assembled the boys as if He were their king; they strewed garments on the ground, and He sat upon them. Then they put on His head a crown wreathed of flowers, and, like attendants waiting upon a king, they stood in order before Him on His right hand and on His left. And whoever passed that way the boys took him by force, crying, "Come hither and adore the King, and then proceed upon thy way."

Arabic *Gospel of the Infancy*

That our Lord Jesus Christ, Son of God and eternal Word, is himself the sole principle of operation of the divine and the human desire Holy Writ abundantly testifies. Beyond that, whether it is necessary to think or to say that on account of his divinity or his humanity there exist in him a single operation or two in no way interests us. We leave such questions to grammarians who sell the results of the word games to children.

Pope Honorius
c.680

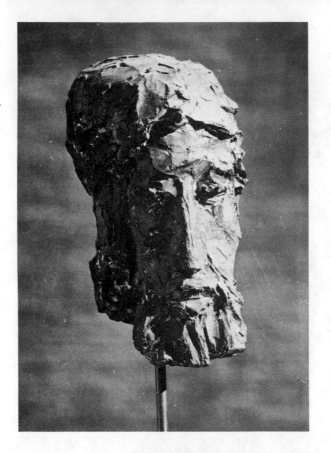

78

I think of Jesus as one who disturbs the very depths of my being. You cannot live in these times and say you're for Jesus when men and women are killing and murdering one another, because the Good News is a Gospel of peace.

Michael Cullen
1942–

Whether Christ was more than a man is a problem. That he was true man, if he was man at all, and that he never ceased to be man, is certain. Consequently the religion of Christ and the Christian religion are two quite different things. The former, the religion of Christ, is that religion which he as a man himself knew and practiced, which every man can have in common with him and which every man must so much the more desire to have in common with him as the character of the man Christ is made more lofty and lovable. The latter, the Christian religion, is that religion which maintains that he was more than a man and as such even makes him the object of its worship. How both of these religions, the religion of Christ, as well as the Christian religion, can exist in Christ as in one and the same person is inconceivable.

Gotthold Ephraim Lessing
c.1775

As far as I am concerned, that rabbi Jesus Christ is nothing more than the first socialist.

Arno Holz
1885

Christ did not choose death, and death on the cross at that, to show the world His love. He was simply killed by men. What touches me about Christ is His giving Himself for others without counting the cost. If He had died to defend an idea, He would have been a hero, but nothing more. Seeing Him on the cross is, for me, a guarantee of the authenticity of His love, but it is not absolutely necessary to convince me of His love.

Juan Arias
1975

I [Cyril] know that they have in mind something more in addition to this. For he who says that the Lord suffered only in the flesh (i.e. and not in the soul) makes the suffering irrational and not endured by the will; but if anyone says that he suffered with rational soul, so that the suffering was of free will, there is no objection to saying that he suffered in his human nature. But if this is true, how are we not to grant that the two natures exist without separation after the union.

Cyril of Alexandria
c.430

In every pang that rends the
  heart
The Man of Sorrows has a
  part.

Michael Bruce
1746-1767

80

Were Jesus suddenly to reappear in the flesh, without fanfare or formality—let us say in a synagogue
in Capernaum . . . it should not seem inconceivable
that the Christian world might find it expedient to
reject Jesus—incredible as this prospect might be—
were he to rebuke Christianity and its established
practices, as he had rebuked the pious Pharisees
and Sadducees for their insincere beliefs and
practices.

David Holland
1968

81

The life of Jesus of Nazareth cannot be discussed in the same way as the life of any other man, however famous. Men like Caesar or Napoleon, for example, had a profound effect on their own age, and may properly be said to have altered the course of history, but none of them ever claimed to give the final and definitive explanation of all that has happened, or will happen, in the course of time. Other men, like the Pharaohs of Egypt, have insisted on being worshipped as gods during their lifetime; but no one takes their claims to divinity seriously today. Quite the contrary is true when we consider the life of Jesus.

Xavier Leon-Dufour
1963

If Christians were Christians, there would be no anti-Semitism. Jesus was a Jew. There is nothing that the ordinary Christian so dislikes to remember as this awkward historical fact. But it happens, nonetheless, to be true.

John Haynes Holmes
1933

'Twas a thief said the last kind word
  to Christ:
Christ took the kindness and forgave
  the theft.

Robert Browning
1812-1889

83

Never to have known Jesus Christ in any way is the greatest of misfortunes, but it involves no perversity or ingratitude. But, after having known Him, to reject or forget Him is such a horrible and mad crime as to be scarcely credible. For He is the origin and source of all good, and just as mankind could not be freed from slavery but by the sacrifice of Christ, so neither can it be preserved but by His power.

Leo XIII
1810-1903

84

Jesus was Jesus because he refused to listen to another and listened at home.

Ralph Waldo Emerson
1803-1882

In these our days appeared a man named Jesus Christ, who yet lives among us, and is accepted as a great prophet of truth by the Gentiles. But His own disciples called Him the Son of God. He has raised the dead and cured all manner of diseases. He is a man of stature somewhat tall and comely, with a ruddy countenance such as one might both love and fear. His hair is the color of a ripe filbert, plain to the ear. It falls down to his shoulders where it is more of an orient color. In the middle of his head is a seam of long hair, after the manner of the Nazarites. His forehead is plain and delicate, the face without blemish or wrinkle, beautiful and comely; His nose and mouth are exactly formed. His beard is the color of His hair and thick, not of much length, but forked. In reproving He is terrible; in admonishing courteous; in speaking, very modest and wise. His body is well-shaped and well-porportioned. None have seen Him laugh; many have seen Him weep. As a man He surpasses in excellence the children of men.

Publius Lentulus,
writing to Caesar and Roman senate

He "became man," that is he took a complete man, (animal) soul and body and rational soul, and all that is man, sins excepted: he was not of human seed, nor in a man, but fashioned for himself flesh to make a holy union, different from his moving, speaking and acting in the prophets, and so became perfect man. For the Word was made flesh, without his own Godhead being changed or transformed into manhood.

Epiphanius of Cyprus
c.370

Like Buddha under the Bo tree, Jesus on his tree, has his eyes closed too. The difference is this. The pain and sadness of the world that Buddha's eyes close out is the pain and sadness of the world that the eyes of Jesus close in.

Frederick Buechner
1926–

85

Jesus was silent, since he felt no pain. . . . [At the end] the Lord cried out, saying, "My power, my power, you have left me." And when he spoke he was taken up.

Apocryphal Gospel of Peter
2nd century

Do you think it was self-denial for the Lord Jesus to come down from heaven to rescue the world: Was it self-denial? No, it was love—love that swallows up everything, and first of all self.

Nikolaus Ludvig von Zinzendorf
to John Wesley
1700-1760

They gave him a manger for a cradle, a carpenter's bench for a pulpit, thorns for a crown, and a cross for a throne. He took them and made them the very glory of his career.

W. E. Orchard
b.1877

Jesus is allotted his place, is called the Son of God, founder of a religion, who sits at the right hand of God. We have molded him to our needs so as to make him readily recognizable, someone we can depend upon, who made a career for himself and achieved something. The truth is that Jesus was not at all reliable. He roused people's anger and provoked unrest, was a stumbling block and caused a scandal. He escapes every attempt to pigeonhole him. He is severe when one might expect him to be mild, yielding where one might expect him to be decisive. He prayed in the temple and yet called for its destruction, upset his own family and then included close relatives in the circle of his disciples. And everywhere he met the question: Who are you? How do we place you? Are you the Messiah? Are you the prophet? Will you restore the kingdom of Israel? In whose authority do you act? Jesus sidestepped all such questions, snapped his fingers at red tape, enjoyed his food and drink where asceticism was expected of him, acknowledged a following but distributed no weapons, spoke of the end of the world but did not forget the priorities of the daily round.

Adolf Holl

Had Christ the death of
   death to death
      Not given death by dying.
The gates of life had never
   been
      To mortals open lying.

                    Epitaph

By a Carpenter mankind was made, and only by
that Carpenter can mankind be remade.

                    Desiderius Erasmus
                    1466-1536

If I could have the table Christ
   Once made in Nazareth,
Not all the pearls in all the sea,
Nor crowns of kings or kings to be
   As long as men have breath,
Could buy that thing of wood He made—
The Lord of Lords who learned a trade.

                    Charles M. Sheldon

88

He does not cease to be God because He becomes Man, nor fail to be Man, because He remains forever God. This is the true faith for human blessedness, to preach at once the Godhead and the manhood, to confess the Word and the flesh, neither forgetting the God, because He is man, nor ignoring the flesh, because He is the Word.

Hilary of Poitiers
368

Christ is clothed with human nature.

Benjamin Whichcote
1609-1683

The Lord applied to Himself two Greek letters, the first and the last, as figures of the beginning and the end which are united in himself. For just as *Alpha* continues on until it reaches *Omega* and *Omega* completes the cycle back again to *Alpha,* so He meant to show us that in Him is found the course of all things from the beginning to the end and from the end back to the beginning, so that every divine dispensation should end in Him through whom it first began, that is, in the Word of God made flesh. Accordingly, it should also end in the selfsame *manner* in which it first began.

Tertullian
160-230

The Divine Man is the great attractive centre, the sole gravitating point of a system which owes to Him all its coherency, and which would be but a chaos were He away.

Hugh Miller

Jesus was not just a moralist whose teaching had some political implications; he was not primarily a teacher of spirituality whose public ministry unfortunately was seen in a political light; he was not just a sacrificial lamb preparing for his immolation, or a God-Man whose divine status calls us to desregard his humanity. Jesus was, in his divinely mandated . . . prophethood, priesthood and kingship, the bearer of a new possibility of human, social, and therefore political relationships.

John H. Yoder
1972

Only once did God choose a completely sinless preacher.

Alexander Whyte
1836-1921

We ought rather choose to have the whole world against us than to offend Jesus. . . . To be without Jesus is a grievous hell, and to be with Jesus a sweet paradise.

Thomas a Kempis
1380-1471

. . . almost you might say like Jesus went into the wilderness to think His way out of a mess of troubles. . . . I ain't saying "I'm like Jesus," the preacher went on. "But I got tired like Him, an' I got mixed up like Him, an' I went into the wilderness like Him, without no campin' stuff."

John Steinbeck
1902-1968

In the blue night
like a black bat
your freaked-out Jesus
hangs to stay:
tired of waiting
centuries for sinners
to shape up,
he droops supine,
bulging, blue,
and gone to fat.

Gerson de Souza
1976

The little flower transplanted to Mount Carmel was to expand under the shadow of the cross. The tears and blood of Jesus were to be her dew, and her Sun was His adorable Face veiled with tears. Until my coming to Carmel, I had never fathomed the depths of the treasures hidden in the Holy Face. . . . He whose Kingdom is not of this world showed me that true wisdom consists in "desiring to be unknown and counted as nothing," in "placing one's joy in the contempt of self." Ah! I desired that, like the Face of Jesus, "my face be truly hidden, that no one on earth would know me." I thirsted after suffering and I longed to be forgotten.

Therese of Lisieux
1873-1897

The Christ head, the Christ face, what man will ever paint, chisel, or carve it? When finished it would float and gleam, cry and laugh, with every other face born human. And how can you crowd all the tragic and comic faces of mankind into one face?

Carl Sandburg
1878-1967

O Lord, how admirable is thy face which a youth will conceive as young, a man as adult, an old man as aged. . . . O face, exceeding comely, whose beauty all who look upon it are unable to admire. Of all faces the face of faces is veiled and seen through a glass darkly, and unveiled is not seen unless one enter above all faces into a certain secret and occult silence where there is nothing of knowledge or concept of a face.

Nicholas of Cusa
1401-1464

The face of Christ does not indeed show us everything, but it shows us the one thing we need to know—the character of God. God is the God who sent Jesus.

P. Carnegie Simpson

93

Is this the face that thrills with awe
    Seraphs who veil their face above?
Is this the face without a flaw,
    The face that is the face of love?
Yea, this defaced, a lifeless clod,
    Hath all creation's love sufficed,
Hath satisfied the love of God,
    This face, the face of Jesus Christ.

        Christina Rossetti
        1830-1894

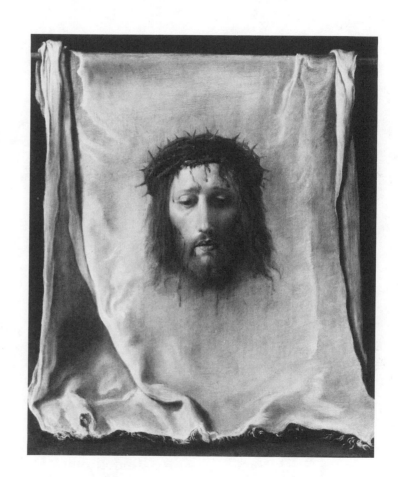

95

I am of the opinion that we should endeavor with all possible zeal to obtain an exact understanding of the great personality of Jesus and to reclaim him for Judaism.

Moritz Lazarus
1824-1903

I do indeed think that we can now know almost nothing concerning the life and personality of Jesus, since the early Christian sources show no interest in either, are moreover fragmentary and often legendary.

Rudolf Bultmann
1958

Do not think that Our Saviour was nailed in the hands, where I have my stigmata. These marks have only a mystical meaning. Jesus must have been fixed more firmly on the cross.

Theresa Neumann

The hands of Christ seem very frail,
For they were broken by a nail.
But only they reach Heaven at last
Whom these frail, broken hands hold fast.

John Richard Moreland

How else but through a broken heart
May Lord Christ enter in?

Oscar Wilde
1856-1900

It is not right to say that the Son proceeded from the Father in the way that living beings are begotten among us, nature from nature with suffering and extreme separation. For the divine is wholly and utterly indivisible, cannot be split, taken apart, cut up, put together or diminished.

Eusebius
c.320

Christ was born of the Virgin, but conceived of the Holy Ghost according to the Scriptures. Christ wept, but according to the scriptures; that which made him weep was also a cause of joy. Christ hungered: but according to the scriptures, he used his power as God against the tree, which bore no fruit, when he had no food. Christ suffered: but according to the scriptures, he was about to sit at the right hand of power. He complained that he was abandoned to die: but according to the scriptures, at the same moment he received in his kingdom in Paradise the thief who confessed him. He died: but according to the scriptures, he rose again and sits at the right hand of God.

Hilary of Poiters
d.368

Perhaps the Christian volume
is the theme,
How guiltless blood for
guilty man was shed,
How He who bore in heaven
the second name
Had not on earth whereon
to lay His head.

Robert Burns
1759-1796

97

And what, then, is there strange in saying that when he [the tempter] beheld Christ's countenance and saw indeed that within he was God, and by nature the true Son of God, and perceived the pure, undefiled, unstained man that surrounded him—a most beautiful, sanctified, inviolable temple—he nonetheless to test him out attacked without hesitation, fighting against God as is his wont.

Eustatius of Antioch
c.330

98

Jesus' fundamental understanding of his mission went far beyond . . . the thought of the humiliation and exaltation of the righteous in contemporary Judaism. It was conditioned by a much more profound consideration—the consciousness of his sonship to the Father, Abba.

A. J. B. Higgins
1964

No one except Christ received the revelations of God without the aid of imagination, whether in words or vision. Therefore the power of prophecy implies not a peculiarly perfect mind, but a peculiarly vivid imagination.

Baruch Spinoza
1632-1677

Therefore, friends,
As far as to the sepulchre of Christ,
Whose soldier now, under whose
   blessed cross
We are impressed and engaged to
   fight . . .
To chase these pagans in those holy
   fields
Over whose acres walk'd those blessed
   feet,
Which fourteen hundred years ago
   were nail'd
For our advantage on the bitter cross.

William Shakespeare
1564-1616

100

O see how Jesus trusts Himself
  Unto our childish love,
As though by His free ways with us
  Our earnestness to prove!

God gives Himself as Mary's Babe
  To sinners' trembling arms,
And veils His everlasting light
  In childhood's feeble charms.

F. Faber
19th century

Christ is not a person for me but a hero, a myth, an extraordinary shadow image in which humanity has painted itself on the wall of eternity.

Hermann Hesse
1919

I meant once to write a book on the background of Christ . . . Galilee and Syria, social, intellectual and artistic of 40 B.C. It would make an interesting book. As good as Renan's *Life of Jesus* should have been, if only he had had the wit to leave out the central figure.

T. E. Lawrence
1888-1935

If Christianity were taught and understood comfortable to the spirit of its Founder, the existing social organism could not exist a day.

Emile Louis Victor de Lavelaye
1822-1892

For the working-class world, Christ seems to be settled with the church and bourgeois society. There is no longer any reason why the worker should encounter Jesus Christ. The church is all one with the fossilized sanctions of the capitalist system. But at this very point, the working class may distinguish between Jesus and his church; *he* is not the guilty party. Up with Jesus, down with the church. Here Jesus can become the idealist, the socialist. What does it mean when, in his world of suspicion and distrust, the worker says, "Jesus was a good man"? It means that there is no need to distrust *him*. The worker does not say, "Jesus is God." But when he says "Jesus was a good man" he is at any rate saying more than when the bourgeois says, "Jesus is God." God for him is something which belongs to the church. But Jesus can be present on the factory floor as the socialist, in politics as the idealist, in the worker's own world as the good man. He fights in their ranks against the enemy, capitalism. Who are you? Are you are brother and Lord? Is the question merely evaded here? Or do they, in their own way, put it seriously?

Dietrich Bonhoeffer
1933

101

The boy Christ of the Gospels is simple and sweet, obedient and humble; He is subject to His parents; He is occupied solely with the quiet duties of His home and of His age; He loves all men, and all men love the pure, and gracious, and noble child. Already He knows God as His Father, and the favor of God falls on Him softly as the morning sunlight or the dew of heaven, and plays like an invisible aureole around His infantile and saintly brow.

Frederick W. Farrar,
Archbishop of Canterbury
1831-1903

Christ, if we call him a philosopher . . . was the poor man's philosopher, the first and only one that has appeared.

Horace Bushnell
1802-1876

Your Saviour comes not with
    gaudy show,
Nor was His kingdom of the
    world below;
The crown He wore was of
    the pointed thorn,
In purple He was crucified,
    not born.

              John Dryden
              1631-1700

Jesus greeted his disciples, saying, "Peace." But
the disciples wondered and were afraid. The Savior
laughed and said to them, "What are you thinking
about? What is perplexing you?"

            The Sophia of Jesus
            4th century
            Gnostic document

Whatever the biblical Christ was, he was not a "do
you own thing" superstar.

            James K. Fitzpatrick

But Thee, but Thee, O sovereign Seer
    of time,
But Thee, O poets' Poet, Wisdom's
    Tongue,
But Thee, O man's best Man, O love's
    best Love.
O perfect life in perfect labor writ,
O all men's Comrade, Servant, King,
    or Priest,—
Oh, what amiss may I forgive in Thee,
Jesus, good Paragon, thou Crystal
    Christ?

            Sidney Lanier
            1842-1881

God bought men here with
His heart's blood expense;
And man sold God here for
base thirty pence.

Robert Herrick
1591-1674

Jesus appears first and foremost as a man among men. If there is one thing that comes across loud and clear in the New Testament it is the fact that Jesus was *a* man. . . . As a man among men he appeared externally to those around him in exactly the same way as any other human individual appears. He experienced fatigue, hunger, disappointment, loneliness and the usual limitations in knowledge that belong to the human condition.

Dermot A. Lane
1975

To be sure, though we were born carnally of Adam, we should nevertheless imitate not him but Christ, in whom we have been reborn and in whom we live when, being renewed to our profit, we lay aside our old way of life. What is it to imitate Adam except to be punished by death for our carnal desires and concupiscences? And what is it to imitate Christ except to be crucified to our carnal concupiscences and desires? In the same way, to lay aside our old way of life is nothing but to live—not according to the flesh, which grows old and dies—but according to God, who alone can continually renew and make happy those who persevere Him.

Julianus Pomperius
c.500

So long as it is recognized that Jesus was a sexual being and had a warm appreciation of marriage, his actual marital status is incidental to his full humanity and to his role as model of Christian morality.

William E. Phipps
1930-

Come down, O Christ, and help me! reach Thy
    hand,
  For I am drowning in a stormier sea
  Than Simon on Thy Lake of Galilee:
Thy wine of life is spilled upon the sand.
My heart is as some famine-murdered land
  When all good things have perished utterly,
  And well I know my soul in hell must lie
If I this night before God's throne should stand.

Oscar Wilde
1856-1900

Jesus, the Son of God, came to us on earth and
brought us the fire of holy love. For this, the very
men to whom he had brought his sacred fire,
nailed him to a cross. But their action did not
quench the fire, but on the contrary caused it to
flame out irresistably.

Anton Sorg
1976

So the body of the Lord is indeed a body, but
incapable of suffering, incorruptible and immortal.
. . . For it is not separated from the Godhead and
belongs to none other than the Only-begotten Son
himself. And it shows us no other person than the
Only-Begotten himself, who is called with our
nature.

Theodoret of Cyprus
c.449

As little as humanity will ever be without religion,
as little will it be without Christ.

David F. Strauss
1808-1874

105

In Jesus' ethos all possible traditions and parallels can be detected and again brought together in unity, but this does not explain the phenomenon of Jesus. And we can emphasize the pre-eminence and universality of love in Jesus' message and bring out the radicality of the theocentrism, of the concentration, intensity, spiritualizing of the ethos of Jesus by comparison—for instance—with Jewish ethics; we can distinguish also the new background of meaning and the new motivations; but we are still far from grasping clearly what is new, unique, about Jesus. What is new and unique about Jesus is the *whole* in its unity; it is this *Jesus himself* in his work.

Hans Küng

There is a common belief among devout people that if we are personally devoted to Christ, His Presence will entirely purify us and put us right in every relation of life. Experience shows that this is simply not true.

William Temple
1881-1944

Without Christ, life is as the twilight with dark night ahead; with Christ it is the dawn of morning with the light and warmth of full day ahead.

Philip Schaff
1819-1893

It is not primarily Jesus' deeds that save man, it is his person. The minute he comes to *be*, man has won a great victory. So, it is better to say that Jesus is reconciliation not that he reconciles. He is the savior, but even more, he is salvation itself. "One-person-in-two-natures" is nothing else than theological shorthand for this pivotal mystery of faith. In Jesus himself, simply by virtue of his existence in our world, salvation and reconciliation take place.

Timothy E. O'Connell

We do not adopt the right point of view in thinking of Christ only as a historical bygone personality. So regarded, the question is asked: what are we to make of his birth, his father and mother, his early domestic relations, his miracles, etc.?—i.e., what is he *unspiritually* regarded? Considered only in respect of his talents, character and morality, as a teacher and so forth, we place him in the same category with Socrates and others, though his morality may be ranked higher. But excellence of character, morality, etc.—all this is not the *ne plus ultra* in the requirements of spirit—does not enable man to gain the speculative idea of spirit for his conceptive faculty. If Christ is to be looked upon only as an excellent, even impeccable individual, and nothing more, the conception of the speculative idea, of absolute truth is ignored. But this is the desideratum, the point from which we have to start. Make of Christ what you will, exegetically, critically, historically—demonstrate as you please, how his doctrines of the church were established by councils, attained currency as the result of this or that episcopal interest or passion, or originated in this or that quarter; let all such circumstances have been what they might—the only concerning question is "what is the idea or the truth in and for itself?"

Georg Wilhelm Hegel
1770-1831

Jesus gave history a new beginning. In every land He is at home: everywhere men think His face is like their best face—and like God's face. His birthday is kept across the world. His deathday has set a gallows against every city skyline, Who is He?

George A. Buttrick
1892–

If Shakespeare should come into this room, we would all rise; but if Jesus Christ should come in, we would all kneel.

Charles Lamb
1775-1834

If Jesus Christ were to come today people would not even crucify him. They would ask him to dinner, and hear what he has to say, and make fun of it.

Thomas Carlyle
1795-1881

The Christ that Harnack sees, looking back through nineteen centuries of Catholic darkness; is only the reflection of a Liberal Protestant face, seen at the bottom of a deep well.

George Tyrrell

Even if liberal Christianity has to give up identifying its belief with the teachings of Jesus in the way it used to think possible, it still has the spirit of Jesus not against it but on its side, Jesus no doubt fits his teachings into the late Messianic dogma, but he does not think dogmatically. He formulates no doctrine. He is far from judging any man's belief by reference to any standard of dogmatic correctness. Nowhere does he demand of his hearers that they shall sacrifice thinking to believing. Quite the contrary! He bids them meditate upon religion. In the Sermon on the Mount he lets ethics, as the essence of religion, flood their hearts, leading them to judge the value of piety by what it makes of a man from the ethical point of view.

Albert Schweitzer
1875-1965

Then God sent his Son, the prince of angels, to men so that he might turn them from their godless and vain cults to the knowledge and worship of the one true God. . . . Now this (Son) remained faithful to God: for he taught that there is only one God and that he alone may be worshipped; and he never named himself God, because (otherwise) he would not have kept faithful, had he (the one who was sent to lead men away from the many gods and to proclaim the one God) introduced any other God besides the One. That would not have been proclamation of the one God who sent him, but the pursuit of his own concern and a separation from the one whom he had come to illuminate. Therefore, because he remained so faithful, because he made no claims for himself, so that he might completely fulfill the task for which he had been sent, he received the rank of eternal priest and supreme king and the authority of judge and the name of God.

Lactantius
c.320

The Son of God goes forth to war,
    A kingly crown to gain;
His blood-red banner streams afar!
    Who follows in His train?

Reginald Heber
1783-1826

111

He did not die with Christian ease,
Asking pardon of His enemies.

William Blake
1757-1827

If Christ has grappled our hearts to Himself at all, then it were surely wise to trust His certainties and not our own doubts, however persistent.

H. H. Farmer

The strange thing about Jesus is that you can ne[ver] get away from Him.

Japanese Stud[ent]

I see Jesus primarily in positive terms. I think [of] him as a man who was literally a man of God[, a] man who was consciously aware of his relations[hip] to a higher destiny and the role which God [had] identified for him as his purpose in life. Throu[gh] the Gospels and through my shared faith w[ith] others, I have come to acknowledge him to be [the] Son of God.

Gary MacE[achern]
1909-

When we read of Jesus' arrest, beware lest we hear and believe the one who tells us that He is arrested as God, that He was arrested despite Himself, arrested because He was powerless. True, He was arrested and bound . . . in the reality of His body; but woe to those who enchain the Word! He is enchained when all we see in Him is a man.

Ambrose
340-397

The Jesus movement has its own catch phrases and slogans—"Smile, Jesus loves you," the ending of sentences with "Praise the Lord" or "Bless you," chants of "Hallelujah" and the "Jesus cheer," "Gimmie a J, gimme an E," etc. There is also a Jesus salute, with one finger pointing skywards from a clenched fist, signifying "One way" (to salvation).

Michael Jacob
1972

Great Prince of heaven! begotten of that King
  Who rules the kingdom that himself did make,
  And of that Virgin Queen man's shape did take,
  Which from king David's royal stock did spring;
No marvel, though thy birth made angels sing,
  And angel's ditties shepherds' pipes awake,
  And kings, like shepherds, humbled for Thy
    sake,
  Kneel at Thy feet, and gifts of homage bring;
For heaven and earth, the high and low estate
  As partners of Thy birth make equal claim;
  Angels, because in heaven God Thee begat.
Shepherds and kings, because Thy Mother came
  From princely race, and yet by poverty
  Made glory shine in her humility.

Henry Constable
16th century

115

116

Christ is not yet risen for the majority of the Latin American people who still suffer misery, starvation and deprivation.

James F. Conway
1971

When Jesus Christ utters a word, He opens His mouth so wide that it embraces all Heaven and earth, even though that word be but in a whisper.

Martin Luther
1843-1546

The Lord professes himself to be the Son of Man, comprising in himself the first man . . . so that through a victorious man we may rise again to life, just as through a vanquished man our human race descended into death. As through a man death obtained victory over us, so again by a man we may attain victory over death.

Irenaeus
c.180

If anyone ventures to say that Christ is a man who bears God (theophoron), and not rather, that He is true God as the one Son in nature, in accordance with the expressions *The Word was made flesh* and *He too shared a common inheritance of flesh and blood* with us, let him be anathema.

Council of Alexandria,
Anathema 5 of St. Cyril
430

He was a gambler too, my Christ,
He took His life and threw it for a world redeemed,
And ere the westering sun went down
Crowning that day with its golden crown,
He knew that He had won.

Unknown

Lowly and meek and mild, they said of Him,
    Mocking Him as he died;
But He was firm of step and straight of limb,
    And tall, and level-eyed—
Young Jesus, turning gallantly to death,
This Man of Nazareth!

Sara Henderson Hay

They nailed Him to the cross,
And He never said a mumblin' word;
They nailed Him to the cross,
And He never said a mumblin' word.
They nailed Him to the cross,
And He never said a mumblin' word—
My Lord, He never said a mumblin' word.

A Spiritual

I tend to see Jesus primarily in terms of his human development and I would see him as not conceiving himself as God but as man. A man who is finding God's call for him and in discovering what God wants of him, he finds that he is God: he proves to be God. . . .

John Dunne
1973

117

The organized charity, scrimped and iced,
In the name of a cautious, statistical Christ.

John Boyle O'Reilly
1844-1890

A theory has been put forward that Jesus never regarded himself as the Messiah and only after his death was he acclaimed as Messiah by his disciples. But had this been true it would never have occurred to his disciples (simple-minded Jews) that one who had suffered crucifixion could be the Messiah; and the messianic idea meant nothing to the Gentile converts. *Ex nihilo nihil fit.* When we see that Jesus' messianic claims became a fundamental principle of Christianity soon after his crucifixion, this is a standing proof that even in his lifetime Jesus regarded himself as the Messiah.

Joseph Klausner

If I had sat at supper with the Lord
  And laid my head upon that saving breast
  I might have turned and fled among the rest—
I might have been the one who left the board
To add the high priest's silver to his hoard.
  Had our Redeemer stopped to wash my feet,
  Would I have washed my neighbor's, clean and
    sweet,
Or thrice denied the Christ I had adored?

Alexander Harvey

This simple peasant from Galilee lived fully as a man of his religion and his times, yet he never allowed his traditional upbringing in the law to shield him from new sources of truth. . . . Pious Jews would scarcely look for the love of God in a common prostitute, but Jesus recognized it there and tried to call it to the attention of Simon and his refined guests.

Kenneth Eberhard

119

The Divine Vision still was seen,
Still was the Human Form Divine,
  Weeping in weak and mortal clay,
O Jesus, still the Form was thine.

William Blake
1757-1827

In Jesus of Nazareth there resides a certain inexhaustibility. I do not know what else to call this feeling which grows as one journeys ever deeper into the Gospel documents. . . . One might as well try to experience the magnitude of the ocean in a thimbleful of salt water as to think once can offer the last word about Jesus. It is not the lack of any "diary" of Jesus but the awesomeness of his moral character and spiritual amplitude that defies a neat, final packaging.

Parker B. Brown

In his life, Christ is an example, showing us how to live; in his death, he is a sacrifice, satisfying for our sins; in his resurrection, a conqueror; in his ascension, a king; in his intercession, a high priest.

Martin Luther
1483-1546

When secular sensibleness has permeated the whole world as it has now begun to do, then the only remaining conception of what it is to be Christian will be the portrayal of Christ, the disciples, and others as comic figures. They will be counterparts of Don Quixote, a man who had a firm notion that the world is evil, that what the world honors is mediocrity or even worse. But things have not yet sunk so deep. Men crucified Christ and called him an enthusiast, etc.—but to make a comic figure of him! Yet this is unquestionably the only logical possibility, the only one, which will satisfy the demands of the age once the secular mentality has conquered. Efforts are being made in this direction—for the world progresses!

Søren Kierkegaard
1813-1855

Today the greatest single deterrent to knowledge of Jesus is his familiarity. Because we think we know him, we pass him by.

Winifred Kirkland
d. 1864

After six years given to the impartial investigation of Christianity, as to its truth or falsity, I have come to the deliberate conclusion that Jesus Christ was the Messiah of the Jews, the Saviour of the world, and my personal Saviour.

Lew Wallace
1827-1905

Thou hast conquered, O pale Galilean!
The world has grown grey from Thy breath.

A. C. Swinburne
1837-1909

Later he saw Jesus move from tree to tree in the back of his mind, a wild ragged figure motioning him to turn around and come off into the dark where he was not sure of his footing, where he might be walking on water and not know it and then suddenly know it and drown.

Flannery O'Connor
1925-1964

No longer . . . may it be said that there is a single view of Jesus that may be labeled "scholarly", and another being equally dubbed "antiquated," or that any one position is, so to speak, in the midstream of scholarly research and all others somewhere on the periphery. Rather, both scholar and lay reader today must face up to the fact that he is being confronted with a number of original and distinctive views of Jesus of Nazareth, all of which may lay claim to be based on adequate scholarship. The problem, the Christian reader finds, is no longer one of knowledge or lack of knowledge of the historical or even archaeological facts involved, nor is it at any rate in most cases a matter of scholarly methodology. . . . The problem today seems, rather, to concern more intangible factors, such as the peculiar bias or motivation or general predilection of the scholar working over the evidence.

John Wick Bowman
1970

121

Hail! Thou Judge of souls departed!
   Hail of all the loving King!
On the Father's right hand throned,
   through His courts Thy praises ring,
Till at last for all offenses righteous
   judgment shalt Thou bring.

> Prudentius
> 4th century

122

When Christ came into my life, I came about like a well-handled ship.

> Robert Louis Stevenson
> 1850-1894

Make it a life-habit to copy the Lord Jesus Christ, the things he did and forbade to do, his life and passion, and think of him at all times as he did for us.

> Meister Johannes Eckhart
> 1260-1328

To my own Gods I go.
It may be they shall give me greater ease
Than your cold Christ and
   tangled Trinities.

> Rudyard Kipling
> 1865-1936

The right faith is this, that we believe and confess that our Lord Jesus Christ, the Son of God, is God and man; God of the substance of the Father; begotten before the worlds; and man of the substance of his mother, born in the world; perfect God and perfect man, of a reasonable soul and human flesh subsisting; equal to the Father in regard to his divinity, and less than the Father in regard to his humanity; who although he be God and man, is still not two but one Christ; one, however, not by conversion of divinity into flesh, but by assumption of humanity into God; wholly one, not by confusion of substance but by unity of person; for as the reasonable soul and flesh is one man, so God and man is one Christ.

> Athanasian Creed

The many Jesuses, not grounded and critiqued by Jesus the Christ of the New Testament, appear playthings, darlings of current concern, usable and disposable figures. They do not carry life or death significance; allegiance to them is not a matter of redemption but of preference. The real danger of the many Jesuses is that they transform Jesus from a two-edged sword into a curiosity piece. In the history of Western Christianity Jesus has been discounted and pushed to the side for many reasons. Today the ultimate discrediting of Jesus is that since nobody knows his name, anybody can call him anything.

John Shea
1975

123

Yea, in the night, my Soul, my daughter
Cry,—clinging Heaven by the hems;
And lo, Christ walking on the water
Not of Gennesareth, but Thames!

Francis Thompson
1859-1907

And I believe that if Christ had not been crucified and had lived out the space which his life had power to cover according to its nature, he would have been changed at the eighty-first year from mortal body to eternal.

Dante Alighieri
1265-1321

Jesus today is at the mercy of a multitude of well-meaning friends who conscientiously seek to do him honor by portraying him in the varied colors of their own immediate religious concerns. To picture him otherwise would seem to diminish his significance for their thinking. Hence they unhesitatingly affirm that the real Jesus has at last been truly discovered in that figure who serves for them as the noblest embodiment of their present ideals. Any suggestion that he may have been primarily concerned with interests different from those characteristic of a modern community, and may have had no desire to pose as a model for all time, is likely to be adjudged beforehand as derogatory to his honor.

Shirley Jackson Case
1932

The sin forgiven by Christ in Heaven
By man is cursed away.

Nathaniel Parker Willis
1806-1867

Since He came in the flesh for the purpose of not only redeeming us by His Passion, but of reaching by us His life, giving and example to those who follow Him, He would not be a King, but freely went to the gibbet of the Cross. He fled from the exalted glory offered Him and chose the pain of an ignominious death, that His members might learn to flee from the favours of the world, not to fear its terrors, to love adversity for the sake of truth, to shrink in fear from prosperity, for this latter thing often defiles the heart by vainglory, but the other cleanses it by sorrow.

Gregory I
540-604

For the early church Jesus was not merely an anonymous rallying point for all sorts of views produced by the growing community. The gospels are certainly determined by the faith of the church, but at the same time they strenuously labor to understand what in the gospels authentically reproduce what Jesus said or did. Yet . . . the distance in the gospels between the Jesus of history and the glorified *Kyrios* strengthens the view that the gospels contain historically valid information about Jesus.

Gustaf Aulen
1879

It may be meaningless coincidence that some young men wear their hair and their feet like the Good Shepherd of the Standard Press Sunday school posters; but there is certainly no randomness to their claim that Jesus was, like themselves, a social critic and an agitator, a drop-out from the social climb, and the spokesman of a counterculture.

John H. Yoder
1972

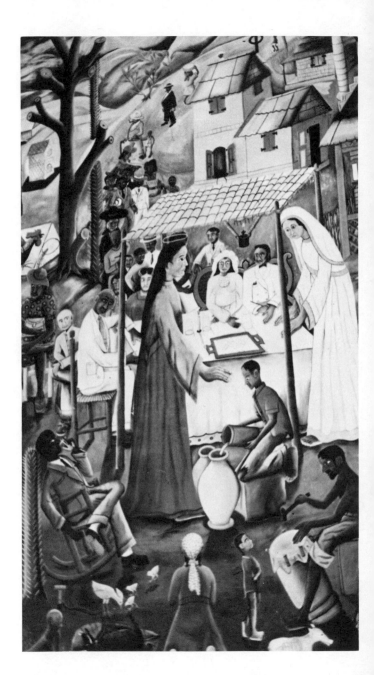

The historical Jesus did not proclaim himself Messiah or Son of God. He did not proclaim his so-called Second Coming, but he did proclaim the imminent coming, if not the actual presence, of the kingdom of God. He particularly sympathized with the poor and the unpopular, the latter including the tax collectors and the Samaritans. He shunned fasting and certain other conventions. He called upon his disciples to be alert for the kingdom of God—described really only obliquely through parables—and to dedicate their lives to it, even to the point of breaking family ties.

John Dart
1976

Get rid of the miracles and the whole world will fall at the feet of Jesus Christ.

Jean Jacques Rousseau
1712-1778

The healing of His seamless dress
Is by our beds of pain;
We touch Him in life's throng and press,
And we are whole again.

John Greenleaf Whittier
1807-1892

127

My advice to you is, take a house next door to the Physician [Christ], for it will be very singular if you should prove to be the very first he ever turned away unhealed.

Samuel Rutherford
1600-1661

As I in hoary winter's night stood
    shivering in the snow,
Surprised I was with sudden heat which
    made my heart to glow;
And lifting up a fearful eye to view
    what fire was near,
A pretty Babe all burning bright did in
    the air appear;
Who, scorched with excessive heat,
    such floods of tears did shed,
As though His floods should quench
    His flames which with His tears
    were fed.

Robert Southwell
16th century

128

I think of Jesus as someone so human that he probably didn't even realize his own divinity, at least in his earlier years. If he fully realized he was God, then somehow the agony in the garden wouldn't come off as real as it should. His crying out to God wouldn't be as real for me.

Ethel Gintoft
1925–

Give us the Christ who can bestow
Some comfort-thought of death.
Give us a Christ our hearts can know—
The Man of Nazareth.

Thomas Curtis Clark

130 Jesus of Nazareth was the most scientific man that ever trod the globe. He plunged beneath the material surface of things, and found the spiritual cause.

Mary Baker Eddy
1821-1910

Jesus Christ and his precepts are found to hit the moral experience of mankind; to hit it in the critical points; to hit it lastingly; and when doubts are thrown upon their really hitting it, then to come out stronger than ever.

Matthew Arnold
1822-1888

[Christ] did not lose his divine power. Even when he hung on the cross, (as God) he bore heaven and earth. Though he hung alongside robbers, he was marvelled at by the angels. Though he was derided by the Jews, he handed over the spirit to the Father. Though he was laid in the tomb, he emptied the rooms of Hades. And though he bore the fetters of the dead, he shattered the bonds of death. Though he was condemned by unbelievers, he will come as judge of the living and the dead. So what use was it for the godless, mere men, to fight against God.

Asterius the Sophist

The figure of the suffering Jesus originated primarily from the need for identification on the part of the suffering masses, and it was only secondarily determined by the need for expiation for the crime of aggression against the father. . . . Dogma developed; the idea of a man becoming a god changes into the idea of a god becoming a man. . . . Jesus eventually became God without overthrowing God because He was always God.

Erich Fromm
1900–

Accordingly, while the distinctness of both natures and substances was preserved, and both met in one person, lowliness was assumed by majesty, weakness by power, mortality by eternity. And, in order to pay the debt of our condition, the inviolable nature was united to the passible, so that as the appropriate remedy for our ills one and the same mediator between God and man, the man Christ Jesus, might from one element be capable of dying and also from the other be incapable. Therefore in the entire and perfect nature of very man was born very God, whole in what was his, whole in what was ours. . . . The Catholic Church lives and goes forward by this faith that in Christ Jesus there is neither humanity without true divinity nor divinity without true humanity.

Leo the Great
390-461

Jesus is certainly a central figure of Jewish history and the history of the Jewish faith, but he is also a part of our present and future, no less than the prophets of the Hebrew Bible whom we can also see not merely in the light of the past.

Schalom Ben-Chorin
1967

Jesus Christ is in the noblest and most perfect sense the realized ideal of humanity.

Johann Gottfried von Herder
1744-1803

It is not shocking, to me at least, to imagine Jesus moved to love according to the flesh. I cannot imagine a *human* tenderness, which the gospels show to be characteristic of Jesus, that is not fed in some degree by the springs of passion. The human alternative to sexual tenderness is not asexual tenderness but sexual fear. Jesus lived in his body, as other men do.

Tom F. Driver
1965

Christ cannot possibly have been a Jew. I don't have to prove that scientifically. It is a fact.

Joseph Paul Goebbels
1897-1945

Jesus Christ is the outstanding personality of all time. . . . No other teacher—Jewish, Christian, Buddhist, Mohammedan—is *still* a teacher whose teaching is such a guidepost for the world we live in. Other teachers may have something basic for an Oriental, an Arab, or an Occidental; but every act and word of Jesus has value for all of us. He became the Light of the World. Why shouldn't I, a Jew, be proud of that?

Sholem Asch
1880-1957

For he had no opposition in his flesh, nor did the strife of desires give rise to a conflict of wishes. His bodily senses were active without the law of sin, and the reality of his emotions being under control of his Godhead and his mind, was neither assaulted by temptations nor yielded to injurious influences.

Leo the Great
390-461

134

The possibility always exists that definitive historical evidence might be produced to show that Jesus was, historically speaking, radically different from the portraits that faith has made of him: that he was a megalomaniac, a guerrilla fighter, a homosexual with compensatory sublimations, a student of Socrates, a man from Mars, or a figment of the phallic mushroom imagination. . . . Many would feel in the face of such a "scientific discovery" that the image of Jesus that is projected across the screen of the Gospels would no longer hold any interest for men. That conclusion does not necessarily follow.

George R. Edwards
1972

God clothed himself in vile man's flesh so He might be weak enough to suffer woe.

John Donne
1572-1631

He is the Good Shepherd, Who gives His life for the sheep—His life for them, His flesh to them, the one for their redemption, the other for their food. O mighty marvel! He is Himself the Shepherd of the sheep, their Pasturage and their redemption's Price.

Bernard of Clairvaux
1091-1153

Jesus strove to heal the breach in man's thinking upon reality, strove to rejoin the divided physical and spiritual realms, saying, poetically, that the energy which gives life to man is, potentially, in a "stone" (Mt. 24). Identifying Himself and mankind with primordial energy, light, He dramatized and phrased in *poetic terms* the most important of the secondary laws of physics, enfolding His answer to the question of the universe in the sign positive (+). His message includes only one mathematical formula and only one mathematically-based law. These are given in word-equations that enfold basic and primary mathematical *axiomata*. How could so much come from an unlearned man —of Nazareth? Who can prove that Jesus was unlearned? But whether by design or because He knew how to tap the fount of truth in His *unconscious* He presented in drama, symbol, and poetry the underlying physical laws that are today being revealed.

Preston Harold
1967

When men looked at Jesus . . . they saw a man who made them realize the dignity of their own humanity. They saw . . . a man on fire with dedication, yet often frustrated; a man who sometimes went hungry and sometimes dined with the rich; a man who amazed crowds, yet lost his own followers. . . . In short, Jesus was a man, *no matter what.*

Leonard Foley

[Jesus] was not educated at court, as Moses apparently was. He was no son of a king like Buddha. Also he was no scholar and politician like Kung-futse [Confucius], nor was he a rich merchant like Mohammed. Precisely because his origin was so insignificant, his lasting importance is so astonishing.

Walter Kaspar
1974

135

Sometime in the reign of Tiberius [*sic*], no one knows exactly where or when, a man appeared who opened a breach in the closed horizon of humanity. He was neither a philosopher nor a ruler, but he lived in such a way that his whole life proclaimed: each one of us can, at any moment, begin a future that is new. . . .

Roger Garaudy
1969

136

Jesus of Nazareth, a Galilean rabbi, whose life marked the watershed of human history, is the key figure of Isaiah's message, as He is the goal of Isaiah's Messianic prophecy. Baruch Spinoza, a Portuguese Jew, called Him ". . . the unrealized ideal of humanity." Only He is capable of getting us all together: Buddhists from the East, Hindus from India and Ceylon, Mohammedans from Africa and western Asia, people of all the residual faiths of China and Japan, pagans from Europe and America, Marxists from everywhere. Unity cannot be achieved by science, government or abstract ideas; what we need is a Messiah! God has already given us one.

Jeane Dixon
1971

The Humanist suggestion that Jesus was "morally right but religiously mistaken" defies all psychological probabilities.

F. R. Barry

Jesus Christ, in fact, is also the Rabbi of Nazareth, historically so difficult to get information about, and when it is obtained, one who is so apt to impress us as a little commonplace alongside more than one other founder of a religion and even alongside many later representatives of His own religion.

Karl Barth
1886-1968

His love at once, and dread,
    instruct our thought;
As man He suffer'd, and as
    God He taught.

Edmund Waller
1606-1687

137

138   If we cannot validly find any revelation of God in the portrait of Jesus as an historical person, how are we ever to reach and accept the dogmas about Him?

D. M. Baillie

[Jesus] is a divine figure sent down from the celestial world of light, the Son of the Most High coming forth from the Father, veiled in earthly form and inaugurating the redemption through his work.

Rudolph Bultmann

There are few Christians who (along with the church fathers themselves) have not fallen into the trap of thinking of Jesus as one who played out a script written by the Father—a script which, thanks to his divinity, he knew and understood well in advance, including how it would all end. We see a haloed Jesus with his friends gathered around him at table, a Jesus who is already virtually risen, in total control of history, including his own.

Tad. W. Guzie
1974

The Gospel writers often say of Jesus, for example, "He did this in order that the prophecy would be fulfilled." As if he knew the script in advance.

John Barth
1966

How do you think the Lord drank when He had become man for our sake? As shamelessly as we do? Was it not rather with good manners and dignity, and leisurely? You are aware, of course, that He, too, took wine: "Take, drink, this is My blood." He used the "blood of the vine" as a figure of the Word who "was shed for us unto the remission of sins," a stream of gladness. From the things he taught about banquets, He plainly insisted that one who drinks must keep self-control. He set the example by not drinking freely Himself. Yet, He proved that what He blessed was really wine when He said to His disciples: "I will not drink of this fruit of the vine, until that day when I shall drink it with you in the Kingdom of My Father."

Clement of Alexandria
190-203

One difference between Christ and other men is this: they do not choose when to be born, but He, the Lord and Maker of history, chose His time, His birthplace, and His mother.

Thomas Aquinas
1225-1274

The sages and heroes of history are receding from us, and history contracts the record of their deeds into a narrower page. But time has no power over the name and deeds and words of Jesus Christ.

William Ellery Channing
1780-1842

Christ had no strife of flesh and spirit which came upon human nature from the transgression of the first man inasmuch as he was born of the Spirit and the Virgin, not through fleshly desire.

Augustine
354-430

[Jesus] had joy, singing its music within, even under the shadow of the cross. It is an unknown word and thing except as He has sway within.

Samuel Dickey Gordon
1859-1936

The most perfect being who has ever trod the soil of this planet was called the Man of Sorrows.

James Anthony Froude
1818-1894

Christ preached the greatness of man. We preach the greatness of Christ. The first is affirmative; the last negative.

Ralph Waldo Emerson
1803-1882

Jesus exists for us . . . as an embodiment of a symbol, a symbol for a specifically Jewish way of looking at the world and mankind.

Vitezslav Gardavsky
1966

The meaning and reality of Christ in any age is not settled by defnition or even by dogmatic pronouncements of bishops in council. Unless the definition clarifies or helps to shape the actual image of Christ of the time, it is an artificial gesture. Further, the present meaning of Christ is not settled by past uses. "Christ" does not mean today what it meant in the first or thirteenth centuries, but its meaning today grows out of what it meant in those periods. In short, the image of Christ has a history, and its present meaning is inseparable from that history.

John B. Cobb, Jr.
1975

It is and remains in any case a surprising phenomenon, after all the fashions falling over one another—not forgetting, in addition to psycho and sensitivity training, the trend toward Far East mysticism—that this Jesus is and becomes constantly freshly relevant, apparently as fascinating as ever. Nor is this any longer Jesus regarded exclusively as a fellow rebel in the fight against war and inhumanity: it is Jesus seen also as the victim abused by everyone, as the most constant and most available symbol for purity, joy, final surrender, true life. And, oddly as some of it may sound to the satisfied bourgeois, could not Jesus' revolution, God-trip, baptism or therapy of the Holy Spirit perhaps be a new expression of a primitive longing of mankind? Of a hunger for true life, true freedom, true love, true peace, which in the long run cannot be suppressed?

Hans Küng

141

The best of men
That e'er wore earth about
   Him was a Sufferer,
A soft, meek, patient, humble,
   tranquil spirit;
The first true gentleman that
   ever breathed.

Thomas Dekker
1570-1641

[After reading St. Matthew's Gospel and his Sermon on the Mount] I began to tell myself that Christ was not the Christ of the pious images, but that he was power, extreme revolt, and that he inflamed. He saved me.

Carlo Coccioli
1955-1956

The real marks of the Jesus revolution are first joy, and happiness in worship, a spirit of happiness. Second, a real commitment to Jesus Christ, to the historic and loving Christ, and to the word of God, the Bible, as the truth. Third, a tremendous compassionate and humanitarian attitude towards our fellow man. Fourth, a great zeal in telling others about Jesus Christ. Fifth, a spirit of victory that has long slipped away from the church.

Arthur Blessitt
1971

As to Jesus of Nazareth, I think His system of morals and His religion, as He left them to us, the best the world ever saw or is like to see; but I apprehend it has received various corrupting changes, and I have, with most of the present dissenters in England, some doubts as to His divinity.

Benjamin Franklin
1706-1790

Christ was the word that
    spake it;
He took the bread and break
    it;
And what that word did
    make it,
That I believe and take it.

Attributed to
Queen Elizabeth I
1533-1603

In Jewish writings—none contemporary with Jesus, some centuries later—we are told these things about Jesus: he was the illegitimate son of a Roman soldier; his mother's name was Mary, and she was a dresser of women's hair; he was a "revolutionary" and he "scoffed at the words of the wise"; he worked miracles by means of magic brought out of Egypt; he had devoted personal disciples, who healed diseases in his name; he was a heretic who sinned and caused the multitude to sin, and he "led astray and deceived Israel"; he was about 33 years-old when he was put to death; and he was executed on the eve of Passover. One thing, however, which the Jewish enemies of Jesus never thought of saying was that he had not existed.

Harry Emerson Fosdick
1949

143

Still as of old
Men by themselves are
     priced—
For thirty pieces Judas sold
Himself, not Christ.

>   Hester H. Cholmondeley
>   19th century

Christ comes to each soul, all trusting as a friend, and in each He is betrayed over and over again.

>   R. H. Benson
>   20th century

No longer do I see the Christchild, I see Christ, the man, the mighty, the glorious man . . . a person with living heartbeats, tempted like ourselves, but victorious . . . a personality.

>   German devotion book
>   1900

145

Lovely was the death
Of Him whose life was Love!
Holy with power,
He on the thought-benighted
Skeptic beamed
Manifest Godhead.

Samuel Taylor Coleridge
1772-1834

Jesus was exasperated and said to the lad, You shall go no further on your way, and the child immediately fell down and died. But some, who saw what took place, said: From whence does this child spring, since his every word is an accomplished deed? And the parents of the dead child came to Joseph and blamed him and said: Since you have such a child, you cannot dwell with us in the village; or else teach him to bless and not to curse. For he is slaying our children. And Joseph called the child aside and admonished him, saying: Why do you do such things that these people must suffer and hate and persecute us? But Jesus replied, I know that these words are not yours; nevertheless for your sake I will be silent. But they shall bear their punishment. And immediately those that had accused him became blind. And those who saw it were greatly afraid and perplexed, and said concerning him: Every word he speaks, whether good or evil, was a deed and became a marvel.

Gospel of Thomas
3rd century

It is neither morally nor exegetically insensible to see in the temple cleansing a revolutionary action on the part of Jesus, if that is not distorted in the direction of Zealotism. In the fact of this paradigm alone, it cannot be intelligently maintained that Jesus passively accepted whatever wrong was perpetrated, even though some would caricature the nonviolence of Jesus by insisting that the non-resistance exemplified in Matthew 5:39 was the sum and total of Jesus' teaching and conduct.

George R. Edwards
1972

I believe in Jesus . . . not just as a great man or a distant historical character but as a living presence who reveals both the Father and the meaning of our lives to us.

Eugene Kennedy
1974

In our own terms, Jesus was a national leader, one of many who as we have seen sprang up among the Jews during their long-drawn-out subjugation by Rome. [The evangelists saw to it that his failure] was piously retouched to smooth away those aspects of Jesus' enterprise that were to prove indigestible to later Christian theory—the violence that attended Jesus' movement, its anti-Roman political implications, and above all, perhaps, its material failure—all were either forgotten or obliterated in the new perspective of Jesus' cultic magnification.

Joel Carmichael
1962

147

An unbroken chain of references to the Essene community by the Dead Sea runs from Rabbi J.'s baptism, on through his teaching, and down to the Last Supper. That being so, how could people so misunderstand J., the sectarian, as to make him the founder of a new universal religion, when all he wanted was to reconcile the chosen people, his people, the Jews, with Yahweh, because the Kingdom of God was at hand? Who made an itinerant Jewish preacher and prophet into the founder of a universal religion that finally clashed with Judaism?

Johannes Lehmann
1971

He was very far removed indeed from the "gentle Jesus meek and mild" whose emasculate representations were so greatly admired in the nineteenth century. . . . Yet Jesus himself, who clearly possessed extraordinary determination, did not refrain from contentiousness at all. On the contrary . . . he gave his Jewish opponents as good as he got from them, and more.

Michael Grant
1977

Jesus did not spend His time guarding the customs; He was sent to His death by the men who did.

Kenneth J. Foreman
1891–

149

The fact that Jesus of Nazareth was coming forward as the Messiah formed the reason why the Sadducees resolved to kill him, and it was not the religious but the political consequences of his claim which they dreaded—the proability that the claim would lead to popular demonstrations, that these demonstrations would provoke the vigorous action of Rome, that the action of Rome would mean the loss of place and power for the Sadducees themselves. It is a baseless idea that the Jews of Palestine as a body, having turned against our Lord because he disappointed their hopes, persecuted him and murdered him.

Anthony C. Deane
1953

. . . if you look into our philosophy you will see that we have taken a lot of Christ's precepts. . . .

Nikita Khrushchev

150

Thus it seems to me that the causes of the death of Jesus emerge quite clearly from the human and scientific point of view (and what is poor science but ignorance disguised!). Many predisposing causes brought it about that He was worn out and physically shattered, when He faced the most terrible torture that malice of men has conceived. One cause was, the determining, immediate and final one, asphyxia.

Pierre Barbet, M.D.
1949

Christ in this country [South Africa] would quite likely have been arrested under the Suppression of Communism Act.

Archbishop Joost De Blank
1963

Wherefore, Christ Jesus, the Son of God, is both God and man. He is God before all ages; man in our own time. He is God because He is the Word of God, for the *Word was God*. But He is man because in His own Person there were joined to the Word a rational soul and a body. Therefore, so far as He is God, He and the Father are one; but so far as He is man, the Father is greater than He. Since He was the only Son of God, not by grace but by nature, in order that he should also be full of grace He became likewise the son of man; and the one selfsame Christ results from the union of both. . . . And thus He became less and still remained equal, being both in one. . . . Being God and man did not make Him two sons of God, but one Son of God: God without beginning, man with a definite beginning—our Lord Jesus Christ.

Augustine
354-430

151

The Gospel, as Jesus proclaimed it, has to do with the Father only and not with the Son.

Adolf Harnack
1900

Oh! say not, heavenly notes
　　To childish ears are vain,
That the young mind at random floats,
　　And cannot reach the strain.

Was not our Lord a little child,
　　Taught by degrees to pray,
By father dear and mother mild
　　Instructed day by day?

John Keble
1904

In [Jesus] contemplation reverts to a commitment not directly temporal, but prophetic and pastoral, with socio-political consequences, more fitted for the ministry of evangelization than for temporal political action.

Segundo Galilea
1974

In the man Jesus God's promise became reality: God became man. He lived at a particular time in a particular country where the culture—under God's guidance—had developed the symbols and concepts which enabled Christ to make himself and his mission understood to simple fishermen. These elements are as inseparable from Christianity as the humanity of Christ is from his divinity. These elements will always be as foreign to the Christians of today in the west as well as in the east. To interpret Christ in terms of Purusha, Narayan, or Vishnu is to turn Christ himself into a symbol of man's self-realization by removing his historical mediacy and all the elements that express it.

Oswald Dijkstra

I tell the Hindus that their lives will be imperfect if they do not also study reverently the teaching of Jesus.

Mahatma Gandhi
1869-1948

153

The difference between Socrates and Jesus Christ? The great Conscious; the immeasurably great Unconscious.

Thomas Carlyle
1795-1881

He who wants to find Christ, must first find the church. How would one know Christ and faith in him if one did not know where they are who believe in him? He who would know something concerning Christ, must neither trust in himself nor build his bridge into heaven by means of his own reason, but he should go to the church; he should attend it and ask his questions there. The church is not wood and stone but the assembly of people who believe in Christ. . . . They certainly have Christ in their midst, for outside the Christian church there is no truth, no Christ no salvation.

Martin Luther
1483-1546

If Jesus had never lived, or if faith in him were shown to be a misunderstanding of the significance of the historical Jesus, then clearly the ground would be taken from under Christian faith. If it lost its support in the historical Jesus, it would perhaps not be simply devoid of an object, but it would lose the object which has always been proclaimed by Christians as the central object of faith.

Gerhard Ebeling
1961

Faith consists in a knowledge of God and of Christ, not in reverence for the church.

John Calvin
1509-1564

I love and venerate the religion of Christ, because Christ came into the world to deliver humanity from slavery, for which God had not created it.

Guiseppe Garibaldi
1807-1882

Sacred infant, all divine,
What a tender love was thine,
Thus to come from highest bliss,
Down to such a world as this.

an old Christmas carol

An undogmatic Christ is the advertisement of a dying faith.

P. T. Forsyth

Simon Peter said to them: Let Mary [Magdalene] go forth from among us, for women are not worthy of the life. Jesus said: Behold, I shall lead her, that I may make her male, in order that she may become a living spirit like you males. For every woman who makes herself male shall enter into the kingdom of heaven.

Gospel of Thomas
4th century Gnostic Document

No teacher ever showed more belief than our Lord in the ordinary man to think rightly, if he be only sincere and open-minded. He did not, except rarely, use the dogmatic method. It would seem as if He feared to stunt men's growth from within thereby.

Charles Gore

I believe we make a big mistake if we portray Jesus Christ too narrowly. To the sick he was a healer. To the hungry he was the feeder. Christ came to men and presented his message in different forms. He is the answer to everyone's needs; it just depends on what you need. I don't see any particular danger in allowing people to view Christ as they wish. I think the danger lies in the fact that we try to limit Christ.

David Du Plessis
1906-

155

If Christ is not divine, every impulse of the Christian world falls to a lower octave, and light and love and hope decline.

Henry Ward Beecher
1813-1887

Christ is of course the firstborn of all humanity, of women as well as men. . . . Nevertheless, the incarnation of the Word took place according to the male sex: this indeed is a question of fact and this fact, while not implying an alleged natural superiority of man over woman, cannot be dis-associated from the economy of salvation: it is indeed, in harmony with the entirety of God's plan as he revealed it, and of which the mystery of the covenant is the nucleus.

Declaration on the Question of the Admission of Women to the Ministerial Priesthood
1977

Jesus told us to see him in the least of his brothers (i.e. everyone) and yet the Vatican can see Jesus only in adult male celibates. The Vatican should be reminded that they are not casting the part of Jesus in a play when they select candidates for ordination.

Yvonne Goulet
1977

He is what we should call an artistic and a Bohemian in His manner of life.

George Bernard Shaw
1856-1950

If Christ comes to rule in the hearts of men, it will be because we take him with us on the tractor, behind the desk, when we're making a sale to a customer, or when we're driving on the road.

Alexander Nunn

If we allow that the divine-human person of Jesus is constituted once and for all through the incarnation, then the history and fate of Jesus—above all his cross and resurrection—have no more constitutive meaning. The death of Jesus is then merely the completion of the incarnation. The resurrection is no more than the confirmation of the divine nature.

Walter Kasper
1974

You maintain that a man, born a human being, and one who suffered the penalty of crucifixion . . . was God, and you believe that he still exists and you worship him in your daily prayers.

Arnobius
early 4th century

Furthermore, I saw that the second Person, who is our Mother substantially—the same very dear Person is now become our Mother sensually. For of God's making we are double: that is to say, substantial and sensual. Our substance is that higher part which we have in our Father, God almighty. And the second Person of the Trinity is our Mother in kind, in our substantial making—in whom we are grounded and rooted; and he is our Mother of mercy, in taking our sensuality. And thus "our Mother" meaneth for us different manners of his working, in whom our parts are kept unseparated. For in our Mother Christ, we have profit and increase; and in mercy he re-formeth and restoreth us: and by the power of his passion, his death and his uprising, oned us to our substance. Thus worketh our Mother in mercy to all his beloved children who are docile and obedient to him.

Julian of Norwich
1342?-1416?

158

Jesus was the one who truly existed for others. His calling was to be the one for the many, whereas the calling of all other men is to let him be that for them: the way, the truth, and the life. He stands apart from all the others also in that he was obedient to his calling, whereas they are not obedient to theirs, or they only learn obedience by relying solely on the obedience of him whom they know and confess as Lord and Savior.

Paul Van Buren
1963

This sublime being who presides over the destiny of the world, we may call divine, not in the sense that Jesus had absorbed all divinity, or has been identical with it, but in the sense that Jesus is he who has caused his fellow men to make the greatest step towards the divine. Mankind in its totality offers to view an assemblage of low and egoistic beings only superior to the animal in that their selfishness is more reflective. But from the midst of this uniform vulgarity there are columns rising toward heaven and bearing witness to a nobler destiny. Jesus is the highest of these columns which show to man whence he comes and whither he must go. . . . His worship will constantly renew its youth, the story of his life will bring ceaseless tears, his sufferings will soften the best hearts, all the ages will proclaim that amongst the sons of men none has been born who is greater than Jesus.

J. Ernest Renan
1823-1892

Two thousand years ago there was One here on this earth who lived the grandest life that ever has been lived yet—a life that every thinking man, with deeper or shallower meaning, has agreed to call divine.

Frederick W. Robertson
1816-1853

We can now see very clearly, as we survey the efforts formerly made to analyze the "life of Jesus," that the enthralling psychological descriptions [of Jesus] mirrored not so much the mentality of Jesus as the spirit of the age in which each of the writers lived. During the Enlightenment, Jesus was seen as a teacher who spoke with great insight of God and virtue. In the age of Romanticism, he appeared as a "religious genius." Where Kantianism was influential, he became an ethical teacher similar to Kant. In times of social upheaval, he was seen as a champion of social reform. And so on.

A New Catechism
1967

O Christ, whose glory fills the heaven,
Our only hope, in mercy given;
Child of a Virgin meek and pure;
Son of the Highest evermore.

Roman Breviary Hymn
Ambrosian, 5th century

The Jesus of the " Lives of Jesus" is nothing but a modern variation of the products of human inventive art, no better than the discredited dogmatic Christ of Byzantine Christology; both are equally far removed from the real Christ.

Martin Kahler
1953

Thou art the Good Shepherd; seek me, a lamb, and do not overlook me in my wanderings.

Byzantine Triodion
8th century

Jesus is the foundation of my whole life. He is my strength. If you have Jesus in your life, you know it, you feel it. He's the solid rock you can stand on every day. There's no problem you can't face if you have the love of Jesus to strengthen you.

Johnny Cash
1932–

The Christ-child stood at Mary's knee,
His hair was like a crown,
And all the flowers looked up at Him,
And all the stars looked down.

G. K. Chesterton
1874-1936

He helped his foster father in the shop, and as Jesus grew tall and strong he assumed more and more of Joseph's work, especially when Joseph's health declined. And when that quiet, faithful man died, there were the thoughts of the son as he stood over all that was left of the man who had given him "legality" and—much more than that—his love. The first adult tears of the human Jesus were shed at this time. But of course in this grief he was not alone. The boy and his Mother were together.

Jim Bishop
1957

When we seek for Jesus in the flesh, we find traces less on earth than in heaven, less in the history books than in folk-myths.

Rudolf Augstein
1972

The vindication of Jesus—the Jesus whose life d
not end with manifest proof of his validity—me
that he who restructures his understanding of C
and of himself on the basis of Jesus can come
terms with his own incompleteness, with the n
validated character of his own existence. He
freed from the compulsion of vindicating himsel
knowing that others do so, and from the dem;
that God vindicate him now. Instead, on the b
of Jesus he ventures to entrust himself and
vindication to God, and is prepared to receiv
where Jesus did—beyond death.

Leander K
1971

You may, however, say of the Lord Jesus Chr
his way was always the highest and that we ou
to follow him in it. That may be true, but our L
should be followed reasonably and not by det;
He fasted forty days: no one is called upon to c
him literally in that. . . . We should take care
follow him intelligently, for he is much more in
on our love than our actions.

Meister Johannes Eckh
1260-1328

Christ risen in the flesh! We must accept the image complete, if we accept it at all. . . . It is only the image of our own experience. Christ rises, when He rises from the dead, in the flesh, not merely as spirit. He rises with hands and feet, as Thomas knew for certain: and if with hands and feet, then with lips and stomach and genitals of a man. Christ risen in the whole of His Flesh, not with some left out.

D. H. Lawrence
1888-1930

I insist that the biblical Jesus proclaimed himself to be the Son of God and the teacher of the word of God to man, not just another prophet or wise man whose offerings could be added to the body of human knowledge as one more slant on things. I insist that an honest reading of the Gospels makes that clear.

James K. Fitzpatrick
1976

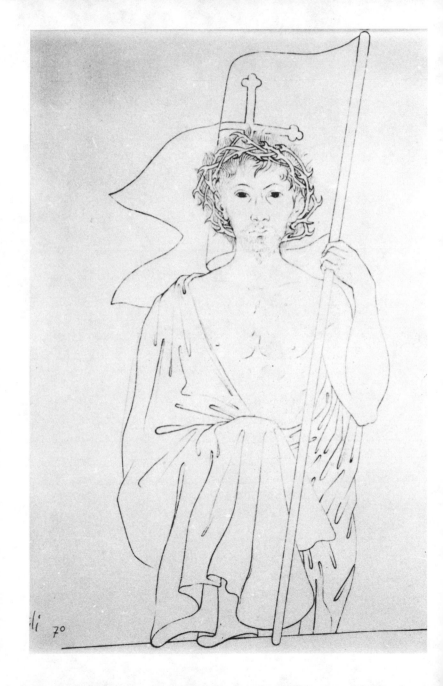

164

Christ is arisen.
  Joy to thee, mortal!
Empty His prison,
  Broken its portal!
Rising, He giveth
  His shroud to the sod;
Risen, He liveth,
  And liveth to God.

J. W. von Goethe
1749-1832

The Christ of Italian filmmaker Dario Fo is far from being the catechism figure of Zeffirelli [*Jesus of Nazareth*]. In the tradition of the *Commedia dell'arte* with its grotesque characters and ribald language, *Mister Buffo* [Fo's series of biblical tales based on the popular traditions of the Middle Ages] presents the Gospel as it was seen by the common people of the Middle Ages. The wedding feast of Cana (a scene Zeffirelli leaves out entirely) is described by an elated drunk, the resurrection of Lazarus by a pick-pocket taking advantage of the crowd gathered to witness the miracle. Using a Lombardian dialect based on the peasant language of the 1400s, Fo creates a Christ who drinks, laughs, eats and dances and talks of the here and now more than the beyond. . . .

Margo Hammond
1977

The true Christ, the divine and heavenly Logos, the only High Priest of the world, the only King of all creation, the only Archprophet of prophets of the Father.

Eusebius
c.320

I mean, Christ was really a very distinguished person, a Prince of the House of David, a poet and an intellectual. Of course He was a carpenter; all those Jews in Bible days could do something with their hands. But what kind of a carpenter was He? Not making cowsheds, I'll bet. Undoubtedly a designer and a manufacturer, in terms of those days. Otherwise, how did He make His connections? You know, when He was travelling around, staying with all kinds of rich and influential people as an honored guest—obviously He wasn't just bumming His way through Palestine; He was staying with people who knew Him as a man of substance who also had a great philosophy. You know, the way those Orientals make their pile before they go in for philosophy.

Robertson Davies
1970

165

166

For it is to the humble-minded that Christ belongs, not to those who exalt themselves above His flock. The Sceptre of the Divine Majesty, the Lord Jesus Christ, did not, for all His power, come clothed in boastful pomp, and everweening pride, but in a humble frame of mind, as the Holy Spirit has told concerning Him.

Clement of Rome
c.96

The dying Jesus is the evidence of God's anger toward sin; but the living Jesus is the proof of God's love and forgiveness.

Lorenz Eifert

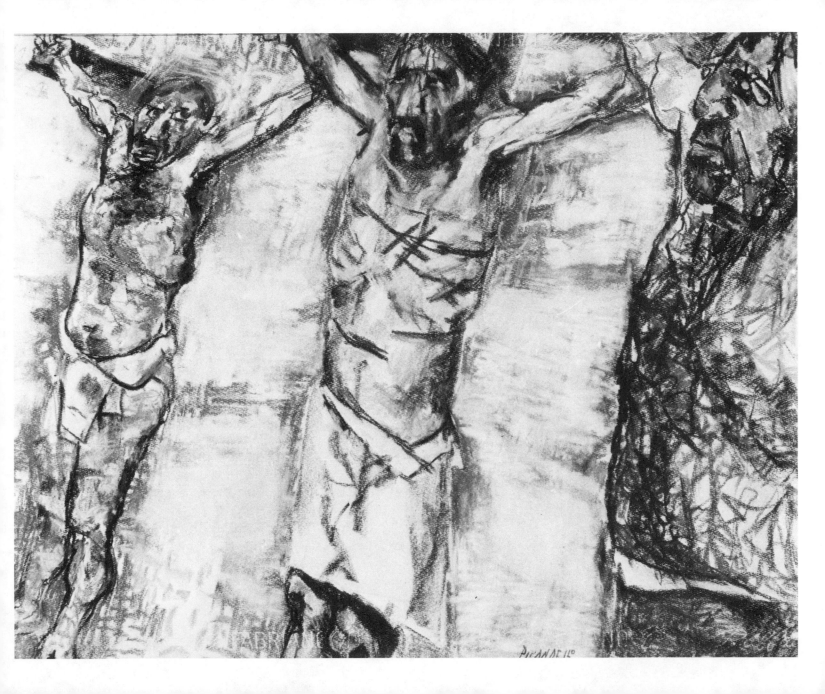

Forsooth, sin is of two kinds; it is either venial or mortal sin. Verily, when man loves any creature more than he loves Jesus Christ our Creator, then is it mortal sin. And venial sin it is if a man love Jesus Christ less than he ought.

Geoffrey Chaucer
1340-1400

Christ has no hands but our hands
    To do His work today;
He has no feet but our feet
    To lead men in His way;
He has no tongue but our tongues
    To tell men how He died;
He has no help but our help
    To bring them to His side.

Annie Johnson Flint

Was Christ a man like us?—Ah! let
  us try
If we then, too, can be such men as he!

Matthew Arnold
1822-1888

Temptation—the Last Temptation—was waiting for him upon the Cross. Before the fainted eyes of the Crucified the spirit of the Evil One, in an instantaneous flash, unfolded the deceptive vision of a calm and happy life. It seemed to Christ that he had taken the smooth, easy road of men. He had married and fathered children. People loved and respected him. Now, an old man, he sat on the threshold of his house and smiled with satisfaction as he recalled the longings of his youth. How splendidly, how sensibly he had acted in choosing the road of men! What insanity to have wanted to save the world! What joy to have escaped the privations, the tortures, and the Cross! . . . But all at once Christ shook his head violently, opened his eyes, and saw. No, he was not a traitor, glory be to God! . . . He reached the summit of sacrifice: he was nailed upon the Cross.

Nikos Kazantazkis

What stands out most . . . in the picture of Jesus is his aloneness. . . . Free of family, he remained alone. He had neither wife nor children. He never clung to any of the companions of his youth, his colleagues, the friends with whom he talked at the doors of the towns he passed. He did not enter into any party, nor any faction. He was not an Essence, not a Pharisee, He would not let himself be classified. He was a solitary man.

Jose Comblin
1976

169

The Lord showed me, so that I did see clearly, that he did not dwell in these temples which men had commanded and set up, but in people's hearts . . . his people were his temple, and he dwelt in them.

George Fox
1624-1691

Jesus was, with the rest of us, a genuine product of the evolutionary process.

John A. T. Robinson

I think that everyone who has gone through a religious conversion feels that they have been saved by Jesus.

Dorothy Day
1897–

He is a path, if any be misled;
　He is a robe, if any naked be;
If any chance to hunger, he is bread;
　If any be a bondman, he is free;
　If any be but weak, how strong is he!
To dead men life is he, to sick men health;
To blind men sight, and to the needy wealth;
A pleasure without loss, a
　treasure without stealth.

Giles Fletcher
1588-1623

And don't you stand around like
　Jesus in Gethsemane.

Bertolt Brecht
1898-1956

Christ was a Person with a mission. One cannot truly love him without also loving what he has at Heart! His love emptied his Heart of even its last drop of blood! Anyone who understands this, and truly loves, is drawn to a similar zeal for souls and unselfish service of others. In fact, zeal for souls and service to our neighbor will always be the best yardstick to judge the authenticity of true devotion to the Sacred Heart.

Walter Kern
1975

171

He is called Jesus by a fitting name, as having the appellation from his salutary healing . . . Jesus means, according to the Hebrew, *Savior,* but in the Greek tongue, *The Healer,* since he is the physician of souls and bodies, curer of spirits, curing the blind body, and leading minds into the light, healing the visibly lame, and guiding the steps of sinners to repentance. . . . If, therefore, anyone is suffering in soul from sins, there is the physician for him.

Cyril of Jerusalem

It is no accident that our Lord was called by the name Jesus. That name sums up the things which he came into the world to do and which only he can do. He came to be the divine Rescuer who alone can deliver men from the consequences and from the grip of sin; he came to be the divine Physician who alone can bring healing to the bodies and the souls of men.

> Jesus! the name that charms our fears,
>   That bids our sorrows cease;
> 'Tis music in the sinner's ears,
>   'Tis life, and health, and peace.

William Barclay
1962

There is one Doctor active in both body and soul, begotten and yet unbegotten, God in man, true Life in death, Son of Mary, and Son of God, first able to suffer and then unable to suffer, Jesus Christ, our Lord.

Ignatius of Antioch
2nd century

And Christ? That is an abyss filled with light. We must close our eyes if we are not to fall into it.

Franz Kafka
1883-1924

Fair is the sunshine,
Fairer still the moonlight,
And all the twinkling starry hosts;
Jesus shines brighter,
Jesus shines purer,
Than all the angels heaven can boast.

German hymn
17th century

We may not go behind the Kerygma, using it as a "source" . . . to reconstruct the "historical Jesus." This would be precisely the "Christ according to the flesh," who is gone. It is not the historical Jesus, but Jesus Christ, the Proclaimed One, who is the Lord.

Rudolf Bultmann
1933

173

The real, i.e. the effective, Christ, who strides through the history of the nations, with whom the great witnesses of the faith have been in communion, struggling, taking, conquering and passing on—*the real Christ is the preached Christ.* And the preached Christ is the Christ in whom men believe.

Martin Kahler
1953

It must be admitted . . . that the jovial Jesus of the Gnostics was less human than the New Testament versions. The Gnostics generally held a "docetic" view of Jesus Christ—that he didn't really suffer on the cross and did not therefore need to be raised from the dead.

John Dart
1976

Matthew presents Jesus as the Royal Savior; Mark, as the Servant of man; Luke, as the Son of man; John, as Son of God.

Anonymous

What the evangelists say through *stories* about what Jesus did for people, we also say through the ritual *action* with bread and wine. Both the stories and the rituals are in their own way interpretations of Jesus; they are different ways of saying who he is for us.

Tad W. Guzie
1974

There is, therefore, only one Christ, who is perfect God and perfect man. We adore Him with the Father and the Spirit together with His immaculate body in one adoration, because for us His body is not unworthy of adoration. In fact, we adore it in the one and only person of the Word who became its person. We do not worship the creature, because we do not adore it as a mere body, but as being one with the divinity, because His two natures belong to the one person of the Word of God. . . . I am not introducing a fourth person in the Trinity, but I do confess the person of the Word of God and of His flesh to be one.

John Damascene
700?-754?

The first fruits of human nature which were taken by the omnipotent Godhead are mingled in the Godhead like a drop of vinegar in a vast sea, but not in its own particular properties. For if the Son were to be known in the ineffable Godhead in a nature of a different kind, identified by its own peculiar characteristics, in such a way that the one were infirm, or small, or corruptible, or transitory, and the other were powerful, and mighty, and incorruptible, and eternal, this would be to postulate two Sons.

Gregory of Nyssa
c.380

Two scientists, using computers, image analyzers and other scientific studies of the Shroud of Turin, have constructed a three-dimensional picture of a figure they believe to be Christ. The two instructors at the U.S. Air Force Academy used photographs of the shroud to obtain a 3-D representation of the image on the shroud. According to their estimates, the man represented on the shroud was five feet, 10 and a half inches tall, weighed about 175 pounds, and had a "Danny Thomas nose."

Newspaper Item
1976

There arose at this time Jesus a Wise man, if it is right to call him a man. For he was a doer of extraordinary acts, a teacher of men who are glad to receive the truth, and he drew to himself many Jews and many of the Greek race. He was the Christ. And when Pilate at the instance of the foremost men among us had sentenced him to be crucified, those who had first loved him did not cease to do so, for on the third day he appeared to them again, alive, since the divine prophets had foretold this and ten thousand other marvels about him. And even now the tribe of Christians named after him is not extinct.

Flavius Josephus
37-100?

The Lord almost always showed Himself to me as risen, also when He appeared in the Host—except at times when He showed me His wounds in order to encourage me when I was suffering tribulation. He appeared on the cross or in the garden, and a few times with the crown of thorns; sometimes He also appeared carrying the cross on account, as I say, of my needs and those of others. But His body was always glorified.

Teresa of Avila
1563-1565

Jesus understood his mission in terms of eschatological prophecy and was confident of its vindication by the Son of man at the End. As eschatological prophet he was not merely announcing the future coming of salvation and judgment, but actually initiating it in his words and works. It is this unexpressed, implicit figure of the eschatological prophet which gives a unity to all of Jesus' historical activity, his proclamation, his teaching with authority, his healings and exorcisms, his conduct in eating with the outcast, and finally his death in the fulfillment of his prophetic mission.

Reginald Fuller
1965

Devotion to the suffering face of Christ in His Passion is rooted in the representation of the face of Christ said to have been left on the towel veil used by Veronica to wipe the face of Jesus. An Archconfraternity of the Holy Face was established in Tours, France, in 1884, whose members make reparation for the blasphemies hurled at Christ.

Maryknoll Catholic Dictionary
1965

Hail, O bleeding Head and wounded,
    With a crown of thorns surrounded,
Buffeted, and bruised and battered,
    Smote with reed by striking shattered,
Face with spittle vilely smeared!
    Hail, whose visage sweet and comely,
Marred by fouling stains and homely,
    Changed as to its blooming color,
All now turned to deathly pallor,
    Making heavenly hosts affeared!

Bernard of Clairvaux
1091-1153

When the symbolism of Jesus stands forth, un-adorned by the reflections of the early church, he is even more challenging than when he is obscured by the theological problems and concerns of primitive Christianity. Jesus was not an ethical teacher or an apocalyptic prophet. He did not think of himself in such a way and did not behave as either rabbis or prophets behaved. His self-understanding and his message were unique, original, and startling. It is small wonder that he shocked and frightened his contemporaries and that they would not accept what he said. It is also small wonder that we have done our best to obscure the shocking nature of the symbolism of Jesus ever since.

Andrew Greeley
1971

Jesus Christ belonged to the true race of prophets. He saw with open eye the mystery of the soul. Drawn by its severe harmony, ravished with its beauty, he lived in it, and had his being there. Alone in all history he estimated the greatness of man. One man was true to what is in you and me. He saw that God incarnates himself in man, and evermore goes forth anew to take possession of his World. He said, in this jubilee of sublime emotion, "I am divine. Through me, God acts; through me, speaks. Would you see God, see me; or see thee, when thou thinkest as I now think." But what a distortion did his doctrine and memory suffer in the same, in the next, and the following ages! There is no doctrine of the Reason which will bear to be taught by the Understanding. The Under-standing caught this high chant from the poet's lips, and said, in the next age, "This was Jehovah come down out of heaven. I will kill you, if you say he was a man." The idioms of his language and the figures of his rhetoric have usurped the place of his truth; and churches are not built on his principles, but on his tropes.

Ralph Waldo Emerson
1803-1882

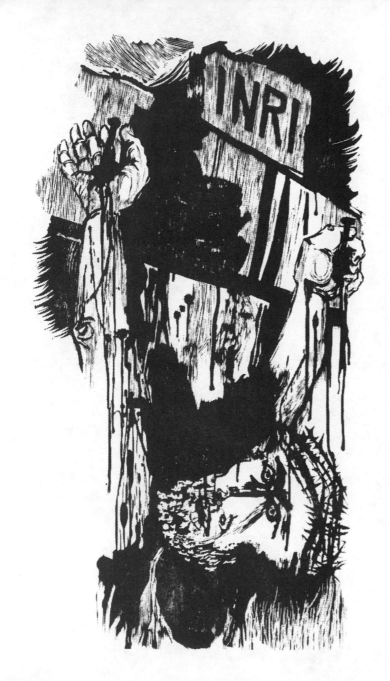

180

The mere thought of Jesus as a married man is felt to be blasphemous by the most conventional believers; and even those of us to whom Jesus is no supernatural personage . . . feel that there was something more dignified in the bachelordom of Jesus.

George Bernard Shaw
1856-1950

The New Testament assumes that Jesus had normal sexuality and sexual desire, both of which are essential for humanness and prerequisite to marriage. . . . In view of no overt evidence to the contrary, it is reasonable that the silence of the New Testament should be interpreted to mean that Jesus internalized the Jewish mores pertaining to sex and marriage.

William E. Phipps
1930–

Christ's life outwardly was one of the most troubled lives that was ever lived: tempest and tumult, tumult and tempest, the waves breaking over it all the time. But the inner life was a sea of glass. The great calm was always there.

Henry Drummond
1851-1897

It is a fact, at any rate, that all the features of the Christ legend connected with this tradition—the hanging from the stake, the piercing with the lance, as well as the sepulchre, resurrection and ascension—were known thousands of years before the birth of Jesus. The figure of *Chrestos* (the Anointed) as the one who would fulfill that heritage of the gods was preprogrammed and prefabricated down to the last detail, and all Jesus really had to do was to carry out "what had been written."

Gerhard Steinhauser
1975

All he did was prompted by love.
Christ, walking the earth,
was the
Sacred Heart of God
opened and opening to all wayfarers.

Francois Mauriac
1885-1970

182

Had there been a Lunatic Asylum in the suburbs of Jerusalem, Jesus Christ would infallibly have been shut up in it at the outset of his public career. The interview with Satan on a pinnacle of the Temple would alone have damned him, and everything that happened after could but have confirmed the diagnosis.

Havelock Ellis
1859-1939

Jesus felt an immovable certainty that *he* was the figure through whom God's purposes were to be fulfilled. This absolute conviction of an entirely peculiar relationship with God was not unknown among Jewish religious leaders, but in Jesus it became a great deal more vigorous and violent than theirs.

Michael Grant
1977

We see that the concept of Jesus held by the early community was that he was a man chosen by God and elevated by him as a "messiah," and later as "Son of God." This Christology of the early community resembles in many respects the concept of the messiah chosen by God to introduce a king-dom of righteousness and love, a concept which had been familiar among the Jewish masses for a long time.

Erich Fromm
1900–

Belief in the resurrection of Jesus is the motive power of all Christian mankind. From what did this faith spring? From five or six remarkably vivid hallucinations? To think so is just as absurd as to suppose that five or six sparks would make water boil in a huge caldron.

Dimitri Merezhkovski
1936–

The poem hangs on the berry bush
    When comes the poet's eye;
The street begins to masquerade
    When Shakespeare passes by.
The Christ sees white in Judas's heart
    And loves His traitor well;
The God, to angel His new heaven,
    Explores His lowest hell.

William Channing Gannett
1840-1923

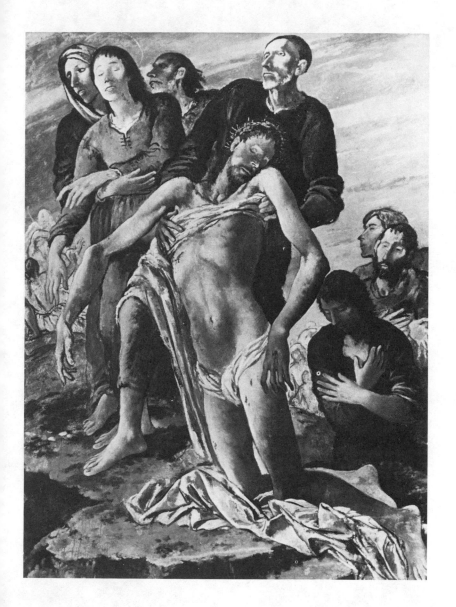

The Christ we find in ourselves is not identified with what we vainly seek to admire and idolize in ourselves—on the contrary, He has identified Himself with what we resent in ourselves, for He has taken upon Himself our wretchedness and our misery, our poverty and our sins. We cannot find peace in ourselves if, in rejecting our misery and thrusting it away from us, we thrust away Christ who loves in us not our human glory but our ignobility.

Thomas Merton
1958

When Jesus tells us about his Father, we distrust him. When he shows us his Home, we turn away, but when he confides in us that he is "acquainted with Grief," we listen, for that is also Acquaintance of our Own.

Emily Dickinson
1830-1886

Jesus is in the world as masked, and the work of the Christian is to strip off the masks of the world to find him, and, finding him, to stay with him and to do his work.

William Hamilton
1966

He [Jesus] was nailed to a tree; he became a fruit of the knowledge of the Father, which did not, however, become destructive because it was eaten, but to those who ate it, it gave cause to become glad in the discovery. . . . They discovered him in themselves—the incomprehensibly inconceivable one, the Father, the perfect one. . . .

Gospel of Truth
4th century

He went about, he was so kind,
   To cure poor people who were blind;
And many who were sick and lame,
   He pitied them and did the same.

Ann and Jane Taylor
1782-1866

We keep emphasizing the way Jesus used miracles as a way of bettering people. Suppose he did it in some other way. Perhaps it is unfortunate that we have a vision of Jesus as a miracle worker. We should remember that he was a slave and what he wanted to do, of course, was to relieve the internal rage of people who have to live in a slave state. That's the thing that's so terrible about it—the rage people experience when they are trapped in some state like that. What Jesus had to do was to salvage the dignity of men who were in a bad situation. I think that is exactly what he did with the Sermon on the Mount, one of the parts of Scripture I think about a great deal. What he said, in effect, was that the slave, by his behavior, could control his enemies, could take their power away. That was an extraordinary insight.

B. F. Skinner
1974

The message of Jesus is addressed to all men. . . .
The liberation which Jesus offers is universal and
integral, it transcends national boundaries, attacks
the foundation of injustice and exploitation, and
186 eliminates politico-religious confusions, without
therefore being limited to a purely "spiritual"
plane.

Gustavo Gutierrez
1971

The humanity of Jesus Christ must never be considered as a garb which God put on to make
himself visible. It is a truly human life, whose
human significance constitutes the key to knowing
the true God.

José Comblin

I have never left the assumed humanity unharmonized with the divine operation, (acting) now as man, now as God, both indicating the nature, and bringing faith to the economy; teaching that the humbler things are to be referred to the humanity, and the nobler to the divinity, and by this unequal mixture of actions, interpreting the unequal union of the natures, and by (my) power over sufferings, declaring that my own sufferings are voluntary; as God, I curbed nature, supporting a fast for forty days, but afterwards, as man, I was hungry and tired; as God, I calmed the raging sea, as man I was tempted by the devil; as God, I expelled devils, as man I am about to suffer for men.

John Chrysostom
345-407

When the grasp upon Christ's divinity is sure and unfaltering, there is no danger that an intimate affection for His humanity will lead souls astray.

R. H. Benson
20th century

187

Fortunately, Christ is greater than the Church.

Ignazio Silone
1968

All men, we believe, tend toward Christ. They do not always seek him in biblical categories. The way men most often seek Christ is in their need for salvation.

Anthony T. Padovano
1934–

If Christ were here now there is one thing he would not be—a Christian.

Mark Twain
1835-1910

Little men, who guarded Jesus' memory [had] drained off the precious life blood of his spirit, mummified his body, . . . wrapped what was left in many foreign wrappings, and over the remains erected a gigantic tomb . . . the Christian Church.

Lewis Mumford
1944

If we turn away from the true Jesus of Nazareth because he has been disfigured and misrepresented by the Churches, we turn away from that in which our weak wills and desponding souls are meant to find their most obvious and natural help and inspiration—from that symbol of the Divine, which, of necessity, means most to us. No! Give him back your hearts—be ashamed that you have ever forgotten your debt to him! Let combination and brotherhood do for the new and simpler faith what they did once for the old—let them give it a practical shape, a practical grip on human life.

Mrs. Humphrey Ward
1851-1920

Future historians . . . are likely to conclude that the more we knew about Jesus the less we knew him, and the more precisely his words were translated the less we understood or heeded them.

Malcolm Muggeridge
1975

Satan. Great acts require great means of enterprise,
Thou art unknown, unfriended, low of birth,
A Carpenter thy Father known, thy self
Bred up in poverty and streights at home;
Lost in a Desert here and hunger-bit:
Which way or from what hope dost thou aspire
To greatness? whence Authority deriv'st,
What Followers, what Retinue canst thou gain,
Or at thy heels the dizzy Multitude,
Longer then thou canst feed them on thy cost?
Money brings Honour, Friends, Conquest,
   and Realms;
What rais'd *Antipater* the *Edomite,*
And his Son *Herod* plac'd on *Juda's* Throne;
(Thy throne) but gold that got him puissant friends?
Therefore, if at great things thou wouldst arrive,
Get Riches first, get Wealth, and Treasure heap,
Not difficult, if thou harken to me,
Riches are mine, Fortune is in my hand;
They whom I favour thrive in wealth amain;
While Virtue, Valour, Wisdom sit in want.
    To whom thus Jesus patiently reply'd:
Yet Wealth without these three is impotent,
To gain dominion or to keep it gain'd.

John Milton
1608-1674

Jesus never claims to be God, personally; yet he always claims to bring God, completely. . . . Jesus is "the man for others."

J. A. T. Robinson

If Jesus were not God, then he deserved an Oscar.

Josh McDowell
1977

191

I do not think Jesus Christ ever existed.

Napoleon I
1769-1821

Christ as God is the fatherland where we are going.
Christ as Man is the way by which we go.

Augustine
354-430

Dear Jesus, Savior of the world,
  Our Savior be today;
Protect our hearts in darkness hurled,
  And guide us in Thy way.

Gregory I
540-604

192

Your glory is dead, oh Christ, and on our cross of
ebony your heavenly corpse has fallen into dust.

Alfred de Musset
1810-1857

There is a view, which is popular with many people today. It recognizes the value of many Christian teachings, but says that Jesus' followers made a god of him after his death. They turned a simple ethical teacher, a Jewish reformer, into a deity; in doing so they betrayed the simple ethics which was the basis of his teaching. Frequently this transformation of Jesus from an ethical itinerant rabbi with reformist learnings into a God-man is blamed on St. Paul.

Louis Michaels
1977

Those who have listened to the Gospels from their childhood believe they can recognize, amid all the cuts and emendations, an unchanging tone which one has only to follow to reach the man Jesus. But the deeper you penetrate, the more indistinguishable this voice becomes in the chorus of other noises. What once was clear breaks down into fugitive colors. *There* is the objection to all scientific theology.

Rudolf Augstein
1972

193

The Savior of our souls and helmsman of our bodies, the Shepherd of the Catholic Church throughout the world.

Martyrdom of St. Polycarp
2nd century

194

It is recognized that Jesus accentuated those distinctive human qualities of freedom, worship, and compassion. Perhaps he should also be admired as one who brought sexuality to full flowering.

William E. Phipps
1930–

Jesus astonishes and overpowers sensual people. They cannot unite Him to history or reconcile Him with themselves.

Ralph Waldo Emerson
1803-1882

There is an image, or a model, which has in it all the qualities that we ascribe to the homosexual, and that's Jesus Christ. I'm not saying that Jesus was a homosexual, mind you. I'm saying that Jesus was a full human being. I'd like to make the point that my ideal type could be either heterosexual or homosexual, as long as one's sexuality doesn't prevent one from developing the fulness of what it means to be human. . . . That's what I mean by Jesus as an ideal—he was a full human being.

John J. McNeill
1976

. . . the Word of God was not changed, but being the same he took a human body for the salvation and well-being of man, that having shared in human birth he might—make man partake in the divine and *reasonable* nature.

Athanasius
293-373

195

The Virgin:
"My lords, see, I hold the Son of God and my
   child in my lap;
He is the One who upholds the whole world."

Gaspar:
"Lady, our very great thanks.
Has anyone ever seen a more beautiful son?"

Mystery Play
15th century

196

The "Jesus Watch"—"Our Savior's likeness . . .
complete with ever-revolving crimson heart . . . in
the race of your choice"—suggests a starting contemporary answer to Jesus' own question in
Matthew's Gospel, "Who do you say the Son of
Man is?" American merchandising in the 70s has
accorded Jesus a place in pop culture alongside
Mickey Mouse, Snow White and Spiro Agnew.
Jesus has become a folk hero, a social phenomenon
and a gimmick to sell timepieces.

Karen Katafiasz DiDomenico

Jesus loves me—this I know,
For the Bible tells me so.

Susan Warner
1860

Mutual in one another's love and wrath all renewing
We live as One Man; for contracting our infinite
   senses
We behold multitude, or expanding we behold as
   one,
As One Man all the Universal Family, and that
   One Man
We call Jesus Christ. . . .

William Blake
1757-1827

If I might comprehend Jesus Christ, I could not
believe in Him. He would be no greater than myself.
Such is my consciousness of sin and inability that I
must have a superhuman Savior.

Daniel Webster
1782-1852

To sum up, Jesus on the Cross is both the symbol and the reality of the immense labor of the centuries which has, little by little, raised the created spirit and brought it back to the depths of Divine Milieu. He represents (and in a true sense, he is) creation, as, upheld by God, it reascends the slopes of being . . . the Cross was placed on the crest of the road which leads to the highest peaks of creation.

Pierre Teilhard de Chardin
1881-1955

Light spoke through [Jesus'] mouth, and his voice gave birth to life. He gave them thought and understanding, and mercy and salvation, and the spirit of power from the infiniteness and gentleness of the Father. . . . He became a way for those who were lost and knowledge for those who were ignorant, a discovery for those who were searching, and a strengthening for those who were wavering, immaculateness for those who were defiled.

Gospel of Truth
4th century

Jesus shall reign where e'er the sun
Does his successive journeys run;
His kingdom stretch from shore to shore
Till moons shall wax and wane no more.

Isaac Watts
1674-1748

Christ is the key to the history of the world. Not only does all harmonize with the mission of Christ, but all is subordinate to it.

Johannes von Muller
1752-1809

The best proof of the historicity of the figure of Jesus which comes down to us is the impossibility of inventing such a figure. Where could anyone find a poet, a novelist, capable of such invention?

José Comblin
1976

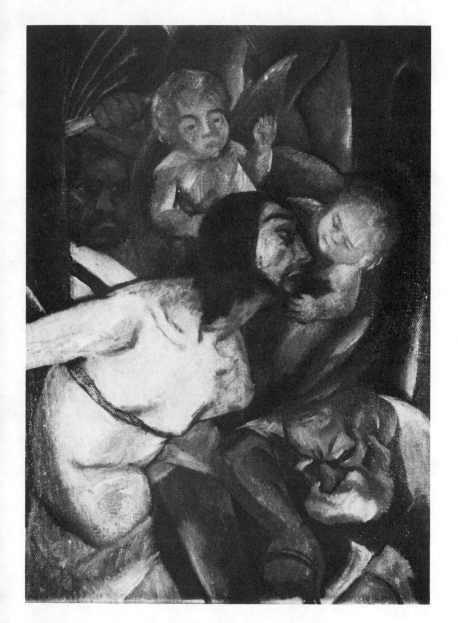

Gentle Jesus, meek and mild,
Look upon a little child;
Pity my simplicity,
Suffer me to come to thee.

Charles Wesley
1707-1788

It is difficult enough for anyone, even a consummate master of imaginative writing, to create a picture of a deeply pure, good person moving about in an impure environment, without making him a prig or a prude or a sort of plaster saint. How comes it that, through all the Gospel traditions without exception, there comes a remarkably firmly-drawn portrait of an attractive young man moving freely about young women of all sorts, including the decidedly disreputable, without a trace of sentimentality, unnaturalness, or prudery, and yet, at every point, maintaining a simple integrity of character?

C. F. D. Monle
1967

The curious and reverent by the thousands have been flocking to [Shamokin, Pennsylvania] to enter a small Episcopal church and witness what appears to be an image of the face of Christ on a tabernacle veil. . . . The image most see is a sorrowful Christ, the outer edges of the veil making up the outer edges of the figure's hair, which flows to the altar. A center fold usually forms the bridge of the nose, with deep eye sockets on both sides where the veil is folded inward casting a shadow. Sometimes darker spots seem to make up eyes and even eyebrows.

Item in *National Catholic Reporter*
1977

Crowds follow'd; thousands shouted, lo, our king!
Fast beat thy heart; now, now the hour draws nigh;
Behold the crown—the throne; the nations bend:
Ah! no, fond mother, no; behold him die.

Harriet Beecher Stowe
1811-1896

The God-Man dies, and thus proves that the incarnation of God is real, that the infinite spirit does not scorn to descend into the lowest depths of the finite, because he knows how to find a way of return into himself, because in the most entire alienation of himself, he can retain his identity.

David F. Strauss
1808-1874

The man, the Christ, the soldier,
Who from His cross of pain
Cried to the dying comrade,
"Lad, we shall meet again."

Willard Wattles
1888-1950

There is a kind of liturgical triumphalism which emphasizes the risen Christ at the cost of the real Jesus who experienced death as we do, and which therefore pulls both the Lord and his supper outside the human condition.

Tad W. Guzie
1974

Our new breed of Jesus Freaks are following the old non-gospel of the freaky Jesus—of the bizarre man who was unnaturally born and whose corpse was weirdly reanimated for a space trip into heaven. But to identify Jesus the man as the one-and-only historical incarnation of a Divinity considered as the royal, imperial and militant Jehovah is only to reinforce the pestiferous arrogance of "white" Christianity—with all the cruel self-righteousness of its missionary zeal.

Alan Watts

Was Jesus charismatic (*pneumatiker*)? The answer is, Yes! And the sense in which he may be called "charismatic" can be fairly clearly defined. He was charismatic in the sense that he manifested a *power* and *authority* which was not his own, which he had neither achieved nor conjured up, but which was given him, his by virtue of the Spirit/power of God upon him. The *power* did not possess him and control him so that he was its instrument willing or unwilling. But neither was he the author of it; nor was he able to dispose of it or ignore it at will. It was a compulsion which filled him, a power which he could exercise in response to faith or which faith could draw through him from its source beyond him. The authority was not his by academic merit or social standing; he has not earned it as a right. And yet it set aside all other authority however sacrosanct, and claimed a hearing before all others, for it came directly from his relationship to God, immediately from his insight into God's will. . . . *It is in terms of this consciousness of power and authority his own and yet not his own, this inspiration immediate and direct from beyond, that Jesus can be called a charismatic.*

James D. Dunn
1975

Many of the saints appeared to the men around them to be great sinners, and many deluded or even wicked men have been held for saints. Christ our Lord, the saint of saints, was criticized as a drunkard and glutton by the holy men of Israel and He was finally put to death by them as a blasphemer because He called Himself Son of God.

Thomas Merton
1958

If ever man was God or God man, Jesus Christ was both.

George Gordon, Lord Byron
1788-1824

203

In the recognition of the royal prerogatives c
Christ and in the return of individuals and c
society to the law of His truth and of His love lie
the only way to salvation.

Pope Pius XI
1876-1958

By His first work He gave me to myself; and by th
next He gave Himself to me. And when He gav
Himself, He gave me back myself that I had lost.

Bernard of Clairvau
1091-1153

I am pretty sure that we err in treating these
sayings as paradoxes. It would be nearer the truth
to say that it is life itself which is paradoxical and
that the sayings of Jesus are simply a recognition of
that fact.

Sir Thomas Taylor
1817-1880

204

You never get to the end of Christ's words. There is
something in them always behind. They pass into
proverbs; they pass into laws; they pass into doctrines; they pass into consolations; but they never
pass away, and after all the use that is made of
them they are still not exhausted.

Arthur P. Stanley
1815-1881

Let me chant in sacred numbers, as I
   strike each sounding string,
Chant in sweet melodious anthems,
   glorious deeds of Christ our King;
He, my Muse, shall be Thy story; with
   His praise my lyre shall ring.

Prudentius
4th century

If contemporary man now perceives reality as personhood-in-relation, then it is in that form that we must cast our vision of the divine originality of Jesus. Jesus is the other-centered man *par excellence,* servant of men and of God.

John H. Yoder
1972

205

Caesar was more talked about in his time than Jesus, and Plato taught more science than Christ. People still discuss the Roman ruler and the Greek philosopher, but who nowadays is hotly for Caesar or against him; and who now are the Platonists and the anti-Platonists? There are still people who love Him and who hate Him. . . . The fury of so many against Him is a proof that He is not dead.

Giovanni Papini
1923

Is it any wonder that to this day this Galilean is too much for our small hearts?

H. G. Wells
1866-1946

206 So crushing was the absurdity of Christ's coming into the world to those who first witnessed that visit, that, from the vantage point of the Cross upon which He met disaster, no man could tolerate His oppressive presence. . . . From that time until now, men slowly straggle back to Calvary, and He must repeat the same unbelievable story. Man has found a way to listen to this terrible tale, but he never gets used to it. How any man can find in Christ the Lord of cosmic order is totally beyond me. He has always presented Himself as the Lord of the Absurd.

Raymond Nogar
1966

Now when we look at Jesus from the point of view of his faith in men, he seems a great skeptic who believes that he is dealing with an evil and adulterous generation, with a people that stones its prophets and then erects monuments to them. He puts no trust in the enduring institutions and traditions of his society. He shows little confidence in his disciples; he is convinced that they will be offended in him, and that the sturdiest of them will be unable to stand by him in the time of testing. Only romantic fictionalizing can interpret the Jesus of the New Testament as one who believed in the goodness of men, and sought by trusting it to bring out what was good in them. Yet despite his skepticism he is remarkably free from anxiety. He is heroic in his faith in God, calling the Lord of heaven and earth Father. He relies in his poverty stricken existence, without family, food, or lodging, on the one who gives the bread needful for the day; and in the end he commends his spirit to Him whom he knows to be responsible for his ignominious and shameful death.

H. Richard Niebuhr
1951

O most merciful Redeemer, Friend, and Brother,
May we know Thee more clearly,
Love Thee more dearly,
Follow Thee more nearly:
For ever and ever.

Richard of Chichester

I know men; and I tell you that Jesus Christ is no
mere man. Between him and every other person in
the world there is no possible term of comparison.
Alexander, Caesar, Charlemagne, and I have
founded empires. But on what did we rest the
creations of our genius? Upon force. Jesus Christ
founded his empire upon love; and at this hour
millions of men would die for him.

Napoleon I
1769-1821

A carpenter has died and left you a fortune.

Church billboard
1977

Jesus, whose lot with us was cast,
Who saw it out, from first to last:
Patient and fearless, tender, true,
Carpenter, vagabond, felon, Jew:
Whose humorous eye took in each phase
Of full, rich life this world displays,
Yet evermore kept fast in view
That far-off goal it leads us to. . . .

Unknown
1938

If I could hear Christ praying for me in the next
room, I would not fear a million enemies. Yet distance makes no difference. He is praying for me.

Robert M. McCheyne
1813-1843

By emphasizing the divine, we may make ourselves too distant from the human Jesus—which is to say, from the only point at which we can honestly begin to understand him, even in his divine aspect. Jesus was not a god who looked like a man (as some Christians seem to present him). He was fully human; if not, his humanity was a trick, an educational device. Christians insisted on this real humanity from the beginning. . . . The paradox of Christianity is that by going into the depths of his humanity Jesus' followers can see his divinity revealed.

208

Louis Michaels
1977

If Christ was really divine, after all, then Judas was merely the instrument of his will. And if Christ was merely a great teacher and prophet who in mid-career fell prey to delusions of grandeur and a persecution complex, then Judas—those 30 pieces of silver aside—was merely doing what he thought was right.

Time magazine
October 25, 1971

JESUS:

This is my blood you drink
This is my body you eat
If you would remember me when you eat and
    drink . . .
I must be mad thinking I'll be remembered—yes
I must be out of my head!
Look at your blank faces! My name will mean
    nothing
Ten minutes after I'm dead!
One of you denies me
One of you betrays me—

Tim Rice

They should have known that he was God. His patience should have proved that to them.

Tertullian
160-230

I have composed in my mind a profession of faith. . . . This is what it is: to believe that there is nothing finer, deeper, more lovable, more reasonable, braver and more perfect than Christ; and, not only is there nothing, but I tell myself with a jealous love, there cannot be anything. More than that: if anyone had told me that Christ is outside truth, and if it had really been established that truth is outside Christ, I should have preferred to stay with Christ rather than with truth.

Fyodor Mikhailovich Dostoyevsky
1821-1881

They had this thing they have at Radio City every year. All these angels start coming out of the boxes and everywhere, guys carrying crucifixes and stuff all over the place, and the whole bunch of them— *thousands* of them—singing "Come All Ye Faithful!" like mad. Big deal. It's supposed to be religious as hell, I know, and very pretty and all, but I can't see anything religious or pretty, for God's sake, about a bunch of actors carrying crucifixes all over the stage. . . . I said old Jesus probably would've puked if He could see it—all those fancy costumes and all. Sally said I was a sacrilegious atheist. I probably am. The thing Jesus *really* would've liked would be the guy that plays the kettle drums in the orchestra.

J. D. Salinger
1919–

Jesus told us to love the young and the old, blacks and whites, the poor and the rich, Catholics, Protestants and Jews. He taught us to live with each other and love one another. Jesus taught us how to live, not die.

Mother Waddles

Plunging into the Life of Christ what seemed to stare at me from the pages of the Gospel was that Christ, the Son of God, did not come into this world to *live*. He came into it to *die*. Death was the goal of His Life, the gold that He was seeking.

Fulton J. Sheen
1895–

The people who hanged Christ never, to do them justice, accused him of being a bore—on the contrary; they thought him too dynamic to be safe. It has been left for later generations to muffle up that shattering personality and surround him with an atmosphere of tedium. We have very efficiently pared the claws of the Lion of Judah, certified him "meek and mild," and recommended him as a fitting household pet for pale curates and pious old ladies. To those who knew him, however, he in no way suggested a milk and water person; they objected to him as a dangerous firebrand. True, he was tender to the unfortunate, patient with honest inquiries, and humble before Heaven; but he insulted respectable clergymen by calling them hypocrites; . . . he went to parties in disreputable company and was looked upon as a "gluttonous man and a wine-bibber, a friend of publicans and sinners"; he assaulted indignant tradesmen and threw them and their belongings out of the Temple; . . . he showed no proper deference for wealth or social position; . . . and he retorted by asking disagreeably searching questions that could not be answered by rule of thumb. He was emphatically not a dull man in his human lifetime, and if he was God, there can be nothing dull about God either.

Dorothy L. Sayers
1893-1957

'Tis midnight; and for others' guilt
    The Man of Sorrows weeps in blood;
Yet He that hath in anguish knelt
    Is not forsaken by His God.

William B. Tappan
1822

Jesus laughed! . . . But how many paintings or statues are there showing a laughing Savior? . . . Where in our devotions are there prayers to a laughing Christ? . . . We seem most easily to recall him as a "man of sorrows," . . . forgetting often how much joy his presence brought children and sinners, tax-collectors, and party-goers, sick and dying. Jesus laughed! . . . We can be sure of that. . . . And he probably laughs at us . . . who rob religion of its playfulness . . . and remember him as a man of tears . . . rather than a person of smiles and laughter.

Carl Pfeifer
1929–

Jesus said unto them: "Who do you say that I am?" And they replied, "You are the eschatological manifestation of the ground of our being, the Kerygma in which we find the ultimate meaning of our interpersonal relationship."
Jesus said unto them: "What?"

Popular saying
1975

When Jesus came to Birmingham, they
    simply passed Him by,
They never hurt a hair of Him, they
    only let Him die.

Geoffrey Anketell Studdert-Kennedy
1883-1929

The history of Jesus remains a piece of quite ordinary history, open to ordinary historical investigation. It does not become a sort of super-history by virtue of the perspective to which it has given rise, nor is the freedom of Jesus beyond all historical comprehension because it has proved to be contagious for the Christian. However closely they may be bound together, both logically and historically, a perspective is a perspective and history is history. In other words, the history of Jesus remains a piece of human history, and the event of Easter and succeeding occasions of conversion are discernment situations.

Paul Van Buren
1963

The Jesus of Nazareth who came forward publicly as the Messiah, who preached the ethic of the Kingdom of God, who founded the Kingdom of Heaven upon earth, and died to give His work its final consecration, never had any existence. He is a figure designed by rationalism endowed with life by liberalism, and clothed by modern theology in an historical garb. This image has not been destroyed from without, it has fallen to pieces, cleft and disintegrated by the concrete historical problems which came to the surface one after another, and in spite of all the artifice, art, artificiality and violence which was applied to them, refused to be planed down to fit the design on which the Jesus of theology of the last hundred and thirty years had been constructed, and were no sooner covered over than they appeared again in a new form.

Albert Schweitzer
1875-1965

Only madness can allow Christianity to begin with Jesus as an historical person.

Franz Overbeck
1903

To say that Jesus in his earthly life knew and judged himself to be God's natural Son and very God is to assert the *unprovable* and, from the perspective of the New Testament, the improbable. Had Jesus known such a thing he *could hardly* have contained his knowledge, yet the gospels are witness that his most intimate disciples did not recognize his essential relation to God prior to the resurrection.

Bruce Vawter
1921–

All hail the power of Jesus' name!
  Let angels prostrate fall;
Bring forth the royal diadem,
  To crown Him Lord of all!

Edward Perronet
1721-1792

All His glory and beauty come from within, and there He delights to dwell, His visits there are frequent, His conversation sweet, His comforts refreshing; and His peace passing all understanding.

Thomas a Kempis
1380-1471

I believe Christ was a man like ourselves; to look upon him as God would seem to me the greatest of sacrileges.

Leo N. Tolstoy
1828-1910

213

But the divine Logos, in no way changed as a result of the fellowship which he has with the body and the soul, without sharing in their weakness, nevertheless imparts to them his Godhead. He becomes one with them and continues in that state in which he was before his entry into that union. This manner of mingling and union is entirely new. The Logos mixes himself and yet always remains unmixed, unconfused, incorrupt and unchanged; he does not share in suffering but only in action.

Nemesius of Emesa
c.400

A question has been raised by contemporary theologians. The humanity of Jesus is just as much an article of faith and just as essential in the Christian teaching about the salvation of man through Christ as the divine sonship of Jesus. Our belief in his mediation is based on his identification with both terms of the saving act. Therefore the church has always rejected heresies which denied the full humanity of Jesus, such as those which proposed that he was an optical illusion, that he was not really born but passed through Mary like a tube, that his suffering and death were merely illusions—to wrap it up in a phrase, that he did not have the full experience of the human condition. The question which has only recently been raised can be put thus: Does the full experience of the human condition include conception by the conjugation of male sperm and female ovum? Is one produced from only one set of chromosomes a fully human being? Matthew and Luke could not have asked these questions. We can and must.

John L. McKenzie
1977

If we assert that the Word of God was born of God in a special way, different from ordinary births, this should be no extraordinary thing to you, who say that Mercury is the angelic Word of God. And if anyone objects that Jesus was crucified [i.e. arguing that gods are not subject to death], in this too he is on a par with those reputed sons of Jupiter of yours who suffered [Aesculapius, Bacchus, Hercules, etc.]. When we affirm that he was born of a virgin, understand this in connection with what you say about Perseus. And when we say that he cured the lame, the paralytic and those born blind, we seem to be talking about deeds very similar to those which Aesculapius is supposed to have done.

Justin Martyr
110-165

215

During the years I have worked with contemporary Jesus research, two words have come to stand out: Jesus as the one who *reveals* and one who *liberates*. Everything that Jesus says and does can be basically described by these two words.

Gustaf Aulen
1879

The cross for the first time revealed God in terms of weakness and lowliness and suffering; even, humanly speaking, of absurdity. He was seen thenceforth in the image of the most timid, most gentle and most vulnerable of all living creatures—a lamb. Agnus Dei!

Malcolm Muggeridge

Little Jesus, wast Thou shy
Once, and just so small as I?
And what did it feel like to be
Out of heaven, and just like me?

Francis Thompson
1859-1907

For Jesus, the liberation of the Jewish people was only one aspect of a universal, permanent revolution. Far from showing no interest in this liberation, Jesus rather placed it on a deeper level, with far reaching consequences.

Gustavo Gutierrez
1971

Almost certainly . . . Joseph died when Jesus was still quite young, and Jesus had to take over the support of his mother and of his younger brothers and sisters, and of the home. . . . Jesus could never have become the Saviour of the world unless he had been the wage-earner of Nazareth. He had to do the little job well, before the big job could be given to him.

William Barclay
1965

216

My Master was a worker,
   With daily work to do,
And he who would be like Him
   Must be a worker too;
Then welcome honest labor,
   And honest labor's fare,
For where there is a worker,
   The Master's man is there.

William George Tarrant
1853

It is lawful to believe that the Christ of history is far inferior to the Christ who is the object of faith.

Proposition condemned by
Decree of Holy Office
1907

Here is a man who was born in an obscure village, the child of a peasant woman. He grew up in another village, and that a despised one. He worked in a carpenter shop for thirty years, and then for three years He was an itinerant preacher. He never wrote a book. He never held an office. He never owned a home. He never had a family. He never went to college. He never put his foot inside a really big city. He never traveled, except in His infancy, more than two hundred miles from the place where He was born. He had no credentials but HIMSELF.

Unknown
early 20th century

Whether or not Jesus actually resembles the mysterious and contradictory figure described in the Gospels (Greek for "good news") is unknowable and unimportant. In fact, it is quite possible that Jesus never existed in history. On the other hand, there is no doubt that the life of the West for nearly two millennia has been dominated by Christianity, that protean yet always somber creed which has not only served beautifully the princes of this world but also afforded occasional solace to those made wretched by their anointed lords.

Gore Vidal
1977

A billion men have since professed his [Christ's] way and never followed it.

Thomas Wolfe
1900-1938

Christ to protect me to-day
  against poison, against burning,
  against drowning, against wounding,
  so that there may come abundance of reward.
Christ with me, Christ before me, Christ behind me,
Christ in me, Christ beneath me, Christ above me,
Christ on my right, Christ on my left,
Christ where I lie, Christ where I sit, Christ where I
  arise,
Christ in the heart of every man who thinks of me,
Christ in the mouth of every man who speaks to me,
Christ in every eye that sees me,
Christ in every ear that hears me.

St. Patrick
389-461

Is it perhaps the time for Jesus slogans? . . . Jesus is always in fashion because he is always real.

Pope Paul VI

JESUS CHRIST
Wanted—For Sedition, Criminal Anarchy, Vagrancy, and Conspiring to Overthrow the Established Government.

Dresses poorly. Said to be a carpenter by trade. Ill-nourished, has visionary ideas, associates with common working people, the unemployed and bums. Alien—believed to be a Jew. Alias: "Prince of Peace," "Son of Man," "Light of the World," etc., etc. Professional Agitator, Red Beard, marks on hands and feet the result of injuries inflicted by an angry mob led by respectable citizens and legal authorities.

first appeared in a Christian
underground paper in U.S.
1969

219

ILLUSTRATIONS

221

222

68 George Grosz, *Maul Halten und Weiterdienen!* (Christ with Gas Mask.) Preussischer Kulturbesitz, Berlin.
69 Sahl Swarz, *Entry Into Jerusalem.* VMCCA.
70 Léon Augustin L'Hermitte, *Christ Visiting the Poor.* Metropolitan Museum of Art, New York. Purchase, 1905, Wolfe Fund.
73 Georg, *Resurrection.* Chapel of Moulin de Vauboyen. Photo: Daniel Frasnay.
74 John DeRosen, *Christ in Majesty.* Courtesy of the National Shrine of the Immaculate Conception, Washington.
77 Max Beckmann, *Christ and the Woman Taken in Adultery.* St. Louis Art Museum. Bequest of Curt Valentin.
78 Virginio Ciminaghi, *Head of Christ.* VMCCA.
79 Abraham Rattner, *Pieta.* VMCCA.
80-81 Catholic Worker House, Los Angeles. Photo: Patty Edmonds, reprinted by permission of the *National Catholic Reporter.*
82 James Ensor, *Entrance of Christ into Brussels* (1898). Etching, printed in brown, 9³/₄" x 14". Collection, The Museum of Modern Art, New York. Abby Aldrich Rockefeller Fund.
84 William Zorach, *Head of Christ* (1940). Stone (peridotite), 14³/₄" high. Collection, The Museum of Modern Art, New York. Abby Aldrich Rockefeller Fund.

87 Aldo Capri, *Christ and Nicodemus.* VMCCA.
90 Gerson de Souza, *Blue Crucifixion,* in *Genius in the Backlands* by Seldon Rodman. Reprinted with permission of the publisher, The Devin-Adair Company.
91A Salvador Dali, *The Sacrament of the Last Supper* (detail). National Gallery of Art, Washington. Chester Dale Collection.
91B Bernard Buffet, *Supper* (detail). VMCCA. Photo: Daniel Frasnay.
93 Hans Moller, *Veronica's Veil,* in *Christian Art.* Courtesy of Denis Paluch, Graphic House, Inc.
94 Albrecht Dürer, *The Sudarium* (The Vernical). Courtesy of The Art Institute of Chicago. The Buckingham Collection.
95 Domenico Fetti, *The Veil of Veronica.* National Gallery of Art, Washington. Samuel H. Kress Collection.
99 William Blake, *The Entombment.* The Tate Gallery, London.
100 Carlo Carra, *Crucifixion.* VMCCA.
102 Aldo Capri, *Christ and the Circus.* VMCCA.
107 Filippino Lippi, *Pieta.* National Gallery of Art, Washington. Samuel H. Kress Collection.
108 Eugene Hall, *The Abandonment,* in *Christian Art.* Courtesy of Denis Paluch, Graphic House, Inc.
110 Thomas Hart Benton, from *Propaganda: The Art of Persuasion in World War II,* by Anthony Rhodes. Reprinted courtesy of Chelsea House Publishers.
112A Ted Neeley as Jesus in *Jesus Christ Superstar,* a Norman Jewison Film. Universal Pictures and Robert Stigwood.

112B Enrique Irazoqui in Pier Paolo Pasolini's *The Gospel According to St. Matthew.* Photo: Angelo Novi.
112C "Judas' Kiss" from Pasolini's *The Gospel According to St. Matthew.*
113A "Jesus and the Children" also from Pier Pasolini's film.
113B Max von Sydow as Jesus in *The Greatest Story Ever Told.* Photo courtesy Cinemabilia, NYC.
114 Floriano Bodini, *Crucifixion.* VMCCA.
116 Marc Chagall, *Christ and the Painter.* VMCCA.
118 Andre Derain, *Last Supper.* Courtesy of The Art Institute of Chicago. Gift of Mrs. Frank R. Lillie.
123 Borgognone, *The Resurrection.* National Gallery of Art, Washington. Samuel H. Kress Collection.
126 Wilson Bigaud, *The Wedding Feast* (detail). Episcopal Cathedral, Port-au-Prince, Haiti. Photo: Anthony Phelps.
129 Ivan Vecenaj, *Conversion of St. Paul.* VMCCA.
132 Howard Ellis, *Boy Jesus in the Temple,* in *Christian Art.* Courtesy of Denis Paluch, Graphic House, Inc.
137 Gabriel Leveque, *Crucifixion.* Collection of Bishop C. Alfred Voegeli.
140 Albrecht Dürer, *The Man of Sorrows.* Courtesy of The Art Institute of Chicago. The Wrenn Collection.
142 David Alfaro Siqueiros, *Christ Mutilated.* VMCCA.

223